T0248309

AMERICAN BOMBER AIRCRAFT OF WORLD WAR II
1941–45

AMERICAN BOMBER AIRCRAFT
OF WORLD WAR II
1941–45

EDWARD WARD

amber
BOOKS

First published in 2024

Published by Amber Books Ltd
United House
London N7 9DP
United Kingdom
www.amberbooks.co.uk
Facebook: amberbooks
Instagram: amberbooksltd
Twitter: @amberbooks
Pinterest: amberbooksltd

ISBN: 978-1-83886-327-2

Editor: Michael Spilling
Additional text: Martin J. Dougherty
Designer: Keren Harragan
Picture research: Terry Forshaw

Printed in China

Contents

Introduction

The bombing aircraft that the United States took to war in 1941 came about as much through bitter interservice rivalries between the US Army Air Corps (USAAC) and the US Navy, including factional infighting within the USAAC itself, as through any systematic technical development.

Likely the most influential single event to take place between the wars, however, was the controversial demonstration of air power arranged by General William 'Billy' Mitchell in 1921 during which a destroyer, cruiser and battleship were sunk by bombers. To the proponents of air power this seemed to suggest that aerial bombardment was rendering earlier forms of warfare obsolete and a group of army officers, with Mitchell at its head, championed a futuristic doctrine predicting that the application solely of daylight precision strategic bombing could remove the enemy's ability to fight by destroying its factories, power supplies and transportation facilities and thus end a war.

'Bomber Mafia'

Over the course of the 1930s this pro-bombing group increased their influence and became known as the 'Bomber Mafia'. Their theory that victory could be achieved through air power alone was boosted by the appearance of such aircraft as the B-10, the high speed of which convinced many Air Corps planners that bombers could successfully attack strategic targets without a fighter escort.

This belief would have profound consequences when US bombers were committed to combat over Europe a decade later, as it became abundantly clear that the day flying bomber could not operate without escort: Eighth Air Force raids simultaneously encountered greater opposition while flying to targets beyond the range of their fighter escorts. As a result, losses mounted, and the widely held belief that the 'combat box' formation adopted by the bomber crews provided sufficient mutual defence to allow the

A B-17 Flying Fortress waist gunner waits before a mission, the ammunition belt of his 12.7mm (0.5in) Browning machine gun loaded and ready. On a B-17, there were two waist gunners located directly opposite one another. Standing near an open window, waist gunners did occasionally suffer from frostbite.

Fortresses and Liberators to operate without escort was proved to be misguided. Matters came to a head in August 1943, during a disastrous mission to bomb factories at Regensburg and Schweinfurt. In total, 376 B-17s took part in the attack, but 60 were shot down (with the loss of 600 airmen killed or captured).

Losses of this magnitude were not tenable, and although wedded to the strategic bombing doctrine ('the bomber will always get through'), the Eighth Air Force temporarily abandoned attacks into Germany beyond the range of Allied fighters. The development of escort fighters had been delayed by the focus on the unescorted bomber, and the appearance of effective types for this role was essentially the result of luck rather than Air Force policy.

The war in Europe seemed to demonstrate that the strategic bomber alone could not win against

an industrially powerful nation and the fighter and tactical bomber still had a crucial part to play.

B-29 success

In the war against Japan, however, the opposite conclusion seemed to emerge: the B-29 was a bomber of unprecedented capability that, while not totally immune from interception, was able to operate over Japan without escort with relative impunity, culminating in the horrifying success of the March 1945 raid on Tokyo, the deadliest air attack ever mounted.

The ultimate combination of B-29 and atomic bomb finally gave the 'Bomber Mafia' the means to end a war by strategic bombing alone, but it had only been the development of this terrifying new weapon that had made it possible. This capability effectively gave the United States Army Air Forces (USAAF) the justification it required to split into an entirely

The B-24J was built in larger numbers than any other member of the Liberator family, and was the only model assembled by all five factories in the B-24 production pool.

independent entity to form the US Air Force (USAF) in September 1947.

Naval bombing aircraft by contrast, followed a different path due to a decision in 1931 to prevent the Navy from operating long-range land-based bombers, restricting them to flying boats and carrier aircraft. Eventually the realities of war saw this policy relaxed and many land bombers, such as the B-24 Liberator and B-25 Mitchell, would see widespread operational service in US Navy hands. Nonetheless the majority of bombing aircraft operated by the US Navy remained the carrier-based torpedo and dive-bombers utilized for fleet operations at sea, and which would be employed so decisively throughout the Pacific theatre.

STRATEGIC BOMBERS

As the spearhead of the US Army Air Forces (USAAF), the heavy strategic bombers were favoured in terms of both planning and production. For example, despite its size and complexity, the B-24 Liberator remains the most-produced US military aircraft in history. The classic B-17 and B-24 led inexorably to the development of the incredible B-29 Superfortress, a design that, when combined with the atomic bomb, fundamentally changed the nature of warfare forever.

The following aircraft are featured in this chapter:

- Douglas B-18 Bolo
- Boeing B-17 Flying Fortress
- Consolidated B-24 Liberator
- Boeing B-29 Superfortress
- Consolidated B-32 Dominator

Operation Tidal Wave – the attack on the Ploesti oil fields in August 1943 – was carried out by 177 B-24 Liberators. The USAAF paid a high price for the raid, with 53 aircraft and 660 air crew lost.

Douglas B-18 Bolo

The B-18 was the most numerous frontline USAAF bomber based overseas when the US entered World War II. Although rapidly superseded by more capable aircraft, the B-18 delivered reliable service in several roles.

Derived from the DC-2 transport, the B-18 was declared the winner in a 1935 competition to select a new bomber for the USAAC (largely due to its relatively low price) and was immediately ordered into production as the B-18 'Bolo', named after a type of Filipino knife.

The first 130 or so B-18s featured a short nose with gun turret mounted above the bombardier's position. However, this turned out to be overly cramped, and the final 217 aircraft were completed to B-18A standard, with the turret relocated to the lower nose and the bombardier housed above this in an enlarged position, resulting in a distinctive pointed snout.

Unremarkable capabilities

The first Bolo-equipped units received the aircraft in the spring of 1937, and with the prospect of war in Europe imminent, Douglas hoped to sell large numbers of B-18s. Unfortunately, the Bolo's performance was too pedestrian to expect to survive in the skies over Western Europe, and the sole overseas order was for 20 examples for the RCAF, which named the aircraft the Digby Mk I, though three US aircraft were also transferred to Brazil. An attempt to improve the Bolo resulted in the significantly redesigned B-23 'Dragon', which possessed much better performance but could not compete with later designs.

The last 38 B-18s on order were built as B-23s and used primarily for training in the US. Many B-18s were destroyed on the ground during the Pearl Harbor attack and in the Philippines, where the aircraft saw considerable use as an armed transport. By mid-1942, the B-18 was being used primarily as an anti-submarine warfare (ASW) platform with the Air Forces Anti-submarine Command (AAFAC), a role in which it proved quite successful, accounting for three U-boats confirmed sunk (one by an RCAF Digby).

Later developments saw the B-18B fitted with radar in the nose and a magnetic anomaly detector (MAD) boom at the tail, the latter feature used in conjunction with rearward-firing rocket-propelled depth charges to detect and attack submarines.

In mid-1943, the USAAF turned over all ASW duties to the Navy, flying PB4Y Liberators, and the RCAF withdrew their Digbys in the same year, though Brazil kept the B-18 operational until 1946.

Douglas B-18B Bolo

Weight (Maximum take-off): 12,552kg (27,672lb)

Dimensions: Length: 17.62m (57ft 10in), Wingspan: 27.28m (89ft 6in), Height: 4.62m (15ft 2in)

Powerplant: Two 746kW (1000hp) Wright R-1820-53 Cyclone nine-cylinder air-cooled radial piston engines

Maximum speed: 346km/h (215mph)

Range: 3380km (2100 miles)

Ceiling: 7285m (23,900ft)

Crew: 6

Armament: One 7.62mm (0.3in) Browning machine gun flexibly mounted in nose, dorsal and ventral positions; up to 2948kg (4400lb) of bombs

---

Douglas B-18B Bolo

Used in the anti-submarine role, the B-18 Bolo could carry up to 2000kg (4400lb) of ordnance. The magnetic anomaly detector (MAD) can be seen fitted to the back of this B-18B.

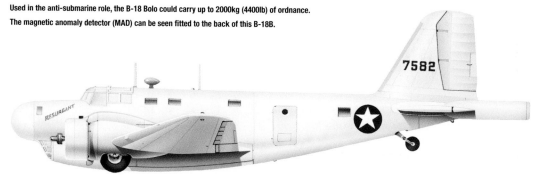

Boeing B-17 Flying Fortress

Probably the most well-known strategic bomber of World War II, the B-17 was originally designed to fulfil a medium bomber contract. Although it achieved fame with the Eighth Air Force in England, the 'Fort' served across the globe in a variety of roles and an impressive 12,731 were built.

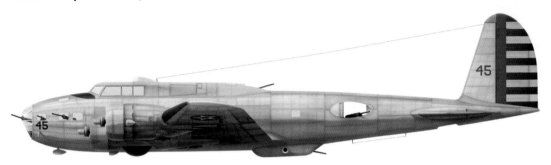

The Boeing Model 299 was designed by a team led by E. Gifford Emery and Edward Curtis Wells to a USAAC specification calling for a 'multi-engine' bomber to replace the innovative twin-engine Martin B-10. This specification was vague enough that Boeing president Claire Egtvedt visited Air Corps officers at Wright Field to confirm that 'multi-engine' could include a four-engined aircraft, as well as the more standard twin. The aircraft was something of a gamble for the then-struggling company. Built at Boeing's own expense, the Model 299 was regarded as a make-or-break undertaking and had it failed to secure an order the future of the company would have been in serious doubt.

After being presented to the press shortly before its first flight on 28 July 1935, its then-unprecedented size, coupled with the profusion of gun positions covering its fuselage, prompted journalist Richard Williams to describe the new bomber as a '15-ton flying fortress' in the *Seattle Times* – delighted with this description, Boeing swiftly trademarked the Flying Fortress

Boeing B-17C Flying Fortress

This B-17C (serial no. 40-2045), flew with the 14th Bombardment Squadron, 7th Bomb Group, Fifth Air Force, from Clark Field, Philippines. Piloted by Captain Colin Kelly, this was the first B-17 to be shot down during the war, on 10 December 1941.

name. The aircraft was also fast; on its delivery flight from Seattle to Wright Field, where the competitive fly-off against the rival Douglas DB-1 and Martin Model 146 was to take place, the Model 299 achieved an impressive average speed of 406km/h (252mph). This was exactly as Boeing had intended when scheming the design; the four-engine layout had been adopted not to improve load-carrying capability – the specification only required a modest 907kg (2000lb) bomb load – but rather to increase speed, and the Model 299 was the fastest of the three competitors by a significant margin.

Early disaster

Demonstrating superior performance to its rivals at the fly-off, the Model

Boeing B-17C

Weight (Maximum take-off): 22,521kg (49,650lb)
Dimensions: Length: 20.67m (67ft 10in), Wingspan: 32.6m (103ft 9in), Height: 4.7m (15ft 5in)
Powerplant: Four 746kW (1000hp) Wright R-1820-65 Cyclone nine-cylinder air-cooled radial piston engines
Maximum speed: 520km/h (323mph)
Range: 3862km (2400 miles)
Ceiling: 12,1390m (37,000ft)
Crew: 9
Armament: One 12.7mm (0.5in) M2 Browning machine gun flexibly mounted in dorsal, ventral and two waist positions; one 7.62mm (0.3in) machine gun could be fired from any of six sockets in the nose; up to 2177kg (4800lb) of bombs

299 was deemed a better fit for the developing USAAC strategic bombing doctrine than the twin-engine designs, but the future of the new bomber was thrown into question when the aircraft was lost in a fatal take-off crash on 30 October 1935. Although not due to any fault in the aircraft itself, the cause was found to be that the control locks had not been released before take-off, rendering the aircraft uncontrollable. The destruction of the

sole Flying Fortress disqualified it from the competition, and the Douglas DB-1 was declared the winner, subsequently entering service as the B-18.

Despite this seemingly terminal setback and the huge unit cost of production aircraft ($99,620 as opposed to $58,200 for the Douglas B-18), the performance of the Model 299 had sufficiently impressed Air Corps officers that a service test batch of 13 aircraft, designated YB-17 (later Y1B-17), was ordered in January 1936. This number was less than Boeing had hoped for but enough to stave off immediate concerns regarding the company's future.

Redesign and innovation

Boeing engineers had been busy since the Model 299's crash improving the design, most significantly replacing the Pratt & Whitney Hornets of the prototype with Wright R-1820 Cyclones of greater power. A significant innovation introduced with the YB-17 to avoid a repeat of the crash that destroyed the prototype was the use of the written pre-flight checklist, an innovation that would subsequently become ubiquitous. An early and much-publicized mission saw three YB-17s,

directed by lead navigator Lieutenant Curtis E. LeMay (later to become the commander of Strategic Air Command), intercept and photograph the Italian Liner Rex 980km (610 miles) off the Atlantic coast. At the same time as the YB-17s were entering service, Boeing modified a 14th example as the first Y1B-17A with turbo-supercharger fitted to all four engines.

Although testing was delayed by teething problems with the new equipment, the turbo-superchargers improved the performance by an order of magnitude. Top speed was raised from 385km/h (239mph) to 501km/h (311mph), and its altitude was improved by a staggering 3.2km (2 miles) over that of the standard Y1B-17. Turbo-supercharged engines were included in the first series production model, the B-17B, of which 39 examples were constructed. These were delivered sporadically as limited funding meant that the Air Corps could afford only to buy a few aircraft at a time. Opposition to the acquisition of further B-17s on the basis of cost largely evaporated in the face of the aircraft's obvious potential coupled with increasing political tensions overseas. An order for over 500 B-17s

was placed in July 1940, though fewer than half of these would be in service by the time of the Pearl Harbor attack.

Bathtub turret

The B-17B was replaced on the production line by the B-17C, which featured more powerful engines and introduced a ventral gondola gun position. Referred to as a 'bathtub turret' by the USAAC, this feature was also retrospectively fitted to several B-17Bs. Internally, the aircraft included self-sealing fuel tanks for the first time along with some armour protection.

Boeing B-17D

Weight (Maximum take-off): 22,521kg (49,650lb)
Dimensions: Length: 20.67m (67ft 10in), Wingspan: 32.6m (103ft 9in), Height: 4.71m (15ft 5in)
Powerplant: Four 746kW (1000hp) Wright R-1820-65 Cyclone nine-cylinder air-cooled radial piston engines
Maximum speed: 512km/h (318mph)
Range: 3862km (2400 miles)
Ceiling: 12,1390m (37,000ft)
Crew: 10
Armament: One 12.7mm (0.5in) M2 Browning machine gun flexibly mounted in each of the two waist positions, two 12.7mm (0.5in) machine guns flexibly mounted in each of the dorsal and ventral positions; one 7.62mm (0.3in) machine gun could be fired from any of six nose sockets; 2177kg (4800lb) of bombs

---

Boeing B-17D Flying Fortress

This B-17D (serial no. 40-3097), nicknamed 'The Swoose', is shown in colours from August 1942. Used extensively in the southwest Pacific, it was the longest serving B-17 in the USAAF, operating from the first day of the war in the Philippines Campaign.

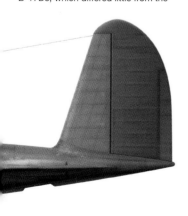

The B-17C would be the first variant to see combat use, though not with US forces, when 20 examples were supplied to the RAF in 1941 and designated the Fortress Mk I, flying their first mission on 8 July 1941. RAF Fortresses flew relatively few sorties as a heavy bomber as the type was not yet truly combat capable and suffered both from manifold mechanical problems as well as heavy losses, with eight having been lost by September. The survivors were transferred to Coastal Command and used successfully as a maritime patrol aircraft. They were subsequently augmented by later variants. Only 38 B-17Cs were built, followed by 42 B-17Ds, which differed little from the

Boeing B-17E Flying Fortress
B-17E-BO (serial no. 41-9019), nicknamed 'Little Skunk Face', served with the 414th Bombardment Squadron, 97th Bomb Group, based at RAF Polebrook, England, September 1942.

C model but did incorporate additional gun positions and feature a revised electrical system.

Mass production
The first mass-produced model of the Flying Fortress was the B-17E, of which 512 would be built. The new model introduced the larger vertical tail surfaces, originally designed for the Boeing Stratoliner airliner, that gave the B-17 its classic profile, after which earlier models were informally known as 'shark fin' variants. The new tail was introduced to cure some directional instability that had been experienced at high altitude, and also featured a gun position for the first time, as it had been found that despite its profusion of defensive weaponry, the Fortress was vulnerable to attack from the rear.

Armament was also enhanced by the addition of a dorsal turret just behind the cockpit, and a remotely sighted ventral turret was added in place of the ventral 'bathtub'. The latter feature proved difficult to use and would only be fitted to initial production B-17Es, with later aircraft receiving a

Boeing B-17E
Weight (Maximum take-off): 25,628kg (56,500lb)
Dimensions: Length: 22.80m (74ft 9in), Wingspan: 32.60m (103ft 9in), Height: 5.85m (19ft 2in)
Powerplant: Four 895kW (1200hp) Wright R-1820-97 Cyclone nine-cylinder air-cooled radial piston engines
Maximum speed: 481km/h (299mph)
Range: 4635km (2880 miles)
Ceiling: 10,975m (36,000ft)
Crew: 10
Armament: One 12.7mm (0.5in) M2 Browning machine guns flexibly mounted in both cheek and waist positions, two 12.7mm (0.5in) M2 Browning machine guns in dorsal and ventral ball turrets and two in tail position, one 7.62mm (0.3in) Browning machine gun flexibly mounted above radio operator's compartment; up to 4355kg (9,600lb) of bombs

retractable manned ball turret in the ventral position.

The addition of this extra armament and its ammunition led to a 20 per cent increase in weight, and the B-17E utilized more powerful Cyclone engines to compensate. The size of the order for B-17Es was too much for Boeing to produce alone, so production was also carried out by the Vega division of Lockheed and at Douglas, the latter company building a new factory specifically to construct B-17s. Flown for the first time in September 1941, B-17Es saw combat on the very first day of the war, when a mixed formation of B-17E and Cs en route to Hickam

Boeing B-17F

CUTAWAY KEY

1 Rudder construction
2 Rudder tab
3 Rudder tab actuation
4 Tail gunner's station
5 Gunsight
6 Twin 12.7mm (0.5in) machine-guns
7 Tailcone
8 Tail gunner's seat
9 Ammunition troughs
10 Elevator trim tab
11 Starboard elevator
12 Tailplane structure
13 Tailplane front spar
14 Tailplane/fuselage attachment
15 Control cables
16 Elevator control mechanism
17 Rudder control linkage
18 Rudder post
19 Rudder centre hinge
20 Fin structure
21 Rudder upper hinge
22 Fin skinning
23 Aerial attachment
24 Aerials
25 Fin leading-edge de-icing boot
26 Port elevator
27 Port tailplane
28 Tailplane leadingedge de-icing boot
29 Dorsal fin structure
30 Fuselage frame
31 Tailwheel actuation
32 Toilet
33 Tailwheel (retracted) fairing
34 Fully-swivelling retractable tailwheel
35 Crew entry door
36 Control cables
37 Starboard waist hatch
38 Starboard waist 12.7mm (0.5in) machine-gun
39 Gun support frame
40 Ammunition box
41 Ventral aerial
42 Waist gunners' positions
43 Port waist 12.7mm (0.5in) machinegun
44 Ceiling control cable runs
45 Dorsal aerial mast
46 Ball turret stanchion support
47 Ball turret stanchion
48 Ball turret actuation mechanism
49 Support frame
50 Ball turret roof
51 Twin 12.7mm (0.5in) machine-guns
52 Ventral ball turret
53 Wingroot fillet
54 Bulkhead
55 Radio operator's compartment
56 Camera access hatch
57 Radio compartment windows (port and starboard)
58 Ammunition boxes
59 Single 7.62mm (0.3in) dorsal machine-gun
60 Radio compartment roof glazing
61 Radio compartment/bomb-bay bulkhead
62 Fire extinguisher
63 Radio operator's station (port side)
64 Handrail links
65 Bulkhead step
66 Wing rear spar/fuselage attachment
67 Wingroot profile
68 Bomb-bay central catwalk
69 Vertical bomb stowage racks (starboard installation shown)
70 Horizontal bomb stowage (port side shown)
71 Dinghy stowage
72 Twin 12.7mm (0.5in) machine-guns
73 Dorsal turret
74 Port wing flaps
75 Cooling air slots
76 Aileron tab (port only)
77 Port aileron
78 Port navigation light
79 Wing skinning
80 Wing leading-edge de-icing boot
81 Port landing light
82 Wing corrugated inner skin
83 Port outer wing fuel tank (nine interrib cells)
84 No. 1 engine nacelle
85 Cooling gills
86 Three-bladed propellers
87 No. 2 engine nacelle
88 Wing leading-edge de-icing boot
89 Port mid-wing (self-sealing) fuel tanks
90 Flight deck upper glazing
91 Flight deck/bombbay bulkhead
92 Oxygen cylinders
93 Co-pilot's seat
94 Co-pilot's control column
95 Headrest/armour
96 Compass installation
97 Pilot's seat
98 Windscreen
99 Central control console pedestal
100 Side windows
101 Navigation equipment
102 Navigator's compartment upper window (subsequently replaced by ceiling astrodome)
103 Navigator's table
104 Side gun mounting
105 Enlarged cheek windows (flush)
106 Ammunition box
107 Bombardier'spanel
108 Norden bombsight installation
109 Plexiglass frameless nosecone
110 Single 12.7mm (0.5in) nose machine-gun
111 Optically-flat bomb-aiming panel
112 Pitot head fairing (port and starboard)
113 D/F loop bullet fairing
114 Port mainwheel 115 Flight deck underfloor control linkage
116 Wingroot/fuselagefairing
117 Wing front spar/fuselage attachment
118 Battery access panels (wingroot leading edge)
119 No. 3 engine nacelle spar bulkhead
120 Intercooler pressure duct
121 Mainwheel well
122 Oil tank (nacelle inboard wall)
123 Nacelle structure
124 Exhaust
125 Retracted mainwheel (semirecessed)
126 Firewall
127 Cooling gills
128 Exhaust collector ring assembly
129 Three-bladed propellers
130 Undercarriage retraction struts
131 Starboard mainwheel
132 Axle
133 Mainwheel oleo leg
134 Propeller reduction gear casing
135 746kW (1,000hp) Wright R-1829-65 radial engine
136 Exhaust collector ring
137 Engine upper bearers
138 Firewall
139 Engine lower bearers
140 Intercooler assembly
141 Oil tank (nacelle outboard wall)
142 Supercharger
143 Intake
144 Supercharger waste-gate
145 Starboard landing light
146 Supercharger intake
147 Intercooler intake
148 Ducting
149 No. 4 engine nacelle spar bulkhead
150 Oil radiator intake
151 Main spar web structure
152 Mid-wing fuel tank rib cut-outs
153 Auxiliary mid spar
154 Rear spar
155 Landing flap profile
156 Cooling air slots
157 Starboard outer wing fuel tank (in inter-rib cut-outs)
158 Flap structure
159 Starboard aileron
160 Outboard wing ribs
161 Spar assembly
162 Wing leadingedge de-icing boot
163 Aileron control linkage
164 Wing corrugated inner skin
165 Wingtip structure
166 Starboard navigation light

This B17F-25-BO Flying Fortress flew with the Eighth Air Force, USAAF, in the European theatre.

SPECIFICATION BOEING B-17F

Crew

Nine, but more could be carried. Crew included: bomb-aimer, pilot, co-pilot, upper turret gunner, radio operator, two waist gunners, ball turret gunner and tail gunner.

Powerplant

Four Wright R-1820-97 Cyclone radial piston engines each rated at 895kW (1200hp) at 7620m (25,000ft)

Performance

Maximum speed: 481km/h (299mph); Cruising speed: 257.5km/h (160mph); Initial climb rate: 274m (900ft) per minute; Service ceiling: 10975m (36,000ft)

Dimensions

Length overall: 22.80m (74ft 9in); Wingspan: 32.60m (103ft 9in); Wing area: 131.92m² (1420 sq ft); Height: 5.85m (19ft 2in); Propeller diameter: 3.54m (11ft 7in)

Armament

Maximum bombload: 4355kg (9,600lb), later increased to (7983kg (17,600lb); defensive firepower normally 10–12 12.7mm (0.5in) guns: two cheek-mounted guns, two on top of fuselage, one above radio operator's compartment, two in 'ball' turret below fuselage, two on hand-operated mountings firing through side ports and two in the extreme tail.

Boeing B-17F Flying Fortress

B-17F-10-BO (serial no. 41-24485), the famous 'Memphis Belle', flew with the 324th Bombardment Squadron, 91st Bomb Group, based at RAF Bassingbourn, UK, May 1942. It was one of the first B-17s to complete 25 combat missions, against targets in occupied France and Germany, during which its gunners shot down eight German aircraft.

Boeing B-17F

Weight (Maximum take-off): 25,628kg (56,500lb)

Dimensions: Length: 22.80m (74ft 9in), Wingspan: 32.60m (103ft 9in), Height: 5.85m (19ft 2in)

Powerplant: Four 895kW (1200hp) Wright R-1820-97 Cyclone nine-cylinder air-cooled radial piston engines

Maximum speed: 481km/h (299mph)

Range: 4635km (2880 miles)

Ceiling: 10,975m (36,000ft)

Crew: 10

Armament: One 12.7mm (0.5in) M2 Browning machine guns flexibly mounted in both cheek and waist positions, two 12.7mm (0.5in) M2 Browning machine guns in dorsal and ventral ball turrets and two in tail position, one 7.62mm (0.3in) Browning machine gun flexibly mounted above radio operator's compartment; up to 7983kg (17,600lb) carried both internally and externally

Field in Hawaii arrived during the Pearl Harbor attack and were attacked by Mitsubishi A6M Zero fighters. Although all 12 aircraft in the formation landed safely, one was so badly damaged that it never flew again, and another was destroyed on the ground.

The B-17E was first used in combat on 2 April 1942, when aircraft from the Seventh Air Force bombed Japanese positions in the Andaman Islands. With this, the B-17E also became the first USAAF Flying Fortress model to arrive in Europe, which would become the type's primary theatre. On 17 August 1942, 12 B-17Es of the Eighth Air

Force bombed marshalling yards at Rouen in France, thus beginning the dogged daylight bombing campaign that would last nearly three years and with which the B-17 would forever be associated. Like the earlier B-17C, the B-17E was also supplied to the RAF, which received 45 examples and designated them the Fortress IIA. The largely unsuccessful use of the earlier Fortress I in daylight raids over Europe meant that these aircraft were not used as bombers by the British but issued directly to Coastal Command squadrons.

Four hundred changes

By the end of the year, the considerably superior B-17F was supplanting B-17Es in frontline squadrons. Easily identified by its new better-streamlined frameless Plexiglas nose, the B-17F otherwise appeared externally identical to the earlier model. Internally, however, some 400 changes had been incorporated into the newer design: uprated Cyclone engines were fitted along with self-sealing oil tanks, additional fuel capacity, an improved oxygen system and an electronic link between the Norden bombsight and the autopilot, allowing the bombardier to control the aircraft via the bombsight on its bombing run and improving accuracy. The B-17F would become the first

Fortress variant to strike Germany itself when, on 27 January 1943, Wilhelmshaven and Emden were attacked. Raids on German targets at ever greater distances and in greater strength led to ever greater losses, and in the absence of a fighter with sufficient range to escort the B-17s to and from targets, an alternative approach was pursued in the form of the remarkable YB-40 gunship.

YB-40

The YB-40 was a modified B-17F that carried no bombs but was fitted instead with a greatly increased gun armament. A second dorsal turret was fitted, and both waist gun positions featured twin 12.7mm (0.5in) machine guns rather than the single gun on stock B-17s. Under the nose, a two-gun Bendix remotely operated chin turret was fitted, controlled from the bombardier's position. The bomb bay was converted to ammunition storage, and all crew positions gained extra armour. 26 YB-40s were eventually completed, some fitted with a variety of experimental armament configurations such as four-gun chin turrets, 40mm (1.57in) cannon and up to 30 handheld machine guns. Fourteen operational missions were flown by the type and were credited with five German fighters shot down for the loss of one YB-40.

Overall, the aircraft was considered a failure, as due to its increased drag and the heavy weight of its ammunition load, it could not keep up with regular B-17Fs – especially once they had dropped their bomb load. With improvements to the range of regular escort fighters, the YB-40 programme was abandoned, though the Bendix chin turret developed for it would be fitted to the last 65 of the 3405 B-17Fs to be completed and would be a distinctive feature of the last and most prolific production model, the B-17G.

B-17G

Flown for the first time on 16 August 1943, the B-17G differed from earlier models in featuring staggered waist gun positions to allow greater freedom of movement for the gunners, another

innovation introduced on the YB-40. The chin gun saw the deletion of the 'cheek' handheld gun positions on either side of the nose in the belief that the new turret possessed sufficient firepower to provide protection in the forward hemisphere. Operational use proved this view unfounded, however, and only the earliest B-17Gs were delivered without the cheek guns.

Late production models introduced the 'Cheyenne' tail gun installation, named after the Cheyenne Modification Center in Wyoming where it had been devised. This allowed the twin 12.7mm (0.5in) tail guns to cover a much greater field of fire than was previously possible, and also saw them equipped with a reflector gunsight for the gunner, replacing

---

Boeing B-17G

Weight (Maximum take-off): 29,700kg (65,500lb)
Dimensions: Length: 22.66m (74ft 4in), Wingspan: 32.60m (103ft 9in), Height: 5.82m (19ft 1in)
Powerplant: Four 895kW (1200hp) Wright R-1820-97 Cyclone radial nine-cylinder air-cooled piston engines
Maximum speed: 462km/h (287mph)
Range: 3219km (2000 miles)
Ceiling: 10,850m (35,600ft)
Crew: 10
Armament: One 12.7mm (0.5in) M2 Browning machine guns flexibly mounted in both cheek and waist positions and above radio operator's compartment, two 12.7mm (0.5in) M2 Browning machine guns in dorsal and ventral ball turrets and two in tail position; up to 7,983kg (17,600lb) carried both internally and externally

---

Boeing B-17G Flying Fortress
B-17G-15-BO (serial no. 42-31353), nicknamed 'Queenie', flew with the 322nd Bombardment Squadron, 91st Bomb Group, based at RAF Bassingborn, UK, April 1944.

Boeing B-17G Flying Fortress
B-17G, named 'Little Miss Mischief', was part of the 324th Bombardment Squadron, 91st Bomb Group, based at RAF Bassingbourn, UK, December 1944.

the somewhat archaic ring and bead sight of the original tail guns. The Cheyenne gun installation was 12.7cm (5in) shorter than the original tail gun position and was retrospectively fitted to many earlier B-17Gs in the field.

Deliveries of the B-17G began in September 1943, and the aircraft was in service in time to supplement the B-17Fs on the second Schweinfurt raid in October 1943. Production of the B-17 was increasing – it would peak in June 1944, when Boeing alone were producing 16 B-17s per day – and large numbers of B-17Gs were available by the spring of 1944. By this time, P-51 Mustangs were available with sufficient range to escort the bombers all the way to Berlin and back, the first such mission being flown in March 1944. The B-17G would continue to attack targets until the end of the war in Europe.

'Mighty Eighth'

The operational peak of the B-17 in the Eighth Air Force service occurred in September 1944, at which point there were 26 operational Bomber Groups based in the UK, all equipped with B-17Gs, and the despatch of 1000

or more Fortresses on a single day's operations had become a relatively commonplace event. The record for the type occurred on Christmas Day 1944, when 1400 B-17Gs attacked airfields and communications in raids across western Germany. In addition to its most famous use with the 'Mighty Eighth', the B-17 also served with the Ninth, Twelfth, and Fifteenth Air Forces in Europe and the Mediterranean, conducting daylight raids across the length and breadth of Europe.

On the other hand, in the Pacific, B-17s were an important type during the initial year of the conflict, although the B-24, with its superior range capability, was better suited to missions in this theatre and had largely supplanted the Fortress by the middle of 1943. The most successful action involving the B-17 in the Pacific was probably the Battle of the Bismarck Sea in March 1943, which saw B-17s bomb and sink three Japanese ships carrying troops to New Guinea and the destroyer Asashio on the following day. Towards the end of the conflict, the Flying Fortress would return to

the Pacific theatre when B-17Gs, redesignated B-17H and later SB-17G, were used to carry and drop lifeboats to aircrew who had been shot down or crashed.

'Aphrodite' flying bomb

The easy flying qualities of the aircraft, described by one pilot as being very much like an enlarged Cessna 172, endeared it to aircrews, and its rock-solid stability was matched by its near-legendary ability to take punishment and remain flying, though the Fortress was not invulnerable. It had an unfortunate tendency to catch fire relatively easily when hit by enemy gunfire, and more B-17s were lost to wing fires than any other cause. The other major flaw of the B-17 was its small bomb load; a legacy of the fact that it had been designed as a medium bomber. The normal bomb load on long-range targets such as Berlin was a mere 1815kg (4000lb), and by February

The Eighth Air Force stopped using camouflage from January 1944, which saved weight, and reflected the USAAF's aerial superiority. These are B-17Gs from the 381st Bomb Group.

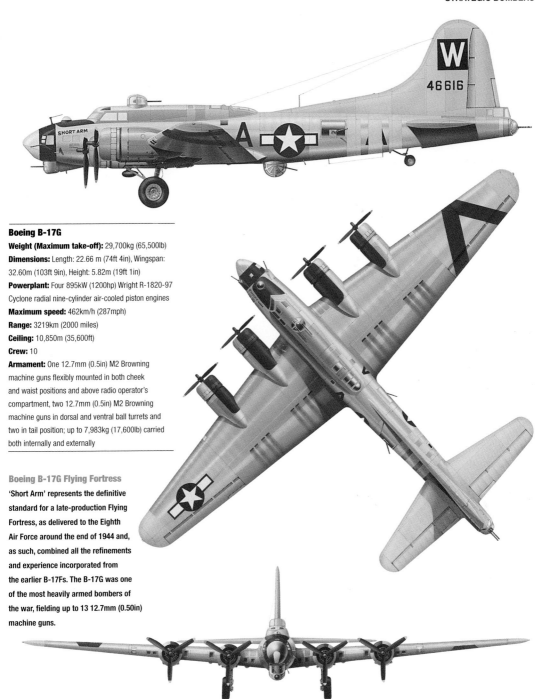

Boeing B-17G

Weight (Maximum take-off): 29,700kg (65,500lb)

Dimensions: Length: 22.66 m (74ft 4in), Wingspan: 32.60m (103ft 9in), Height: 5.82m (19ft 1in)

Powerplant: Four 895kW (1200hp) Wright R-1820-97 Cyclone radial nine-cylinder air-cooled piston engines

Maximum speed: 462km/h (287mph)

Range: 3219km (2000 miles)

Ceiling: 10,850m (35,600ft)

Crew: 10

Armament: One 12.7mm (0.5in) M2 Browning machine guns flexibly mounted in both cheek and waist positions and above radio operator's compartment, two 12.7mm (0.5in) M2 Browning machine guns in dorsal and ventral ball turrets and two in tail position; up to 7,983kg (17,600lb) carried both internally and externally

Boeing B-17G Flying Fortress

'Short Arm' represents the definitive standard for a late-production Flying Fortress, as delivered to the Eighth Air Force around the end of 1944 and, as such, combined all the refinements and experience incorporated from the earlier B-17Fs. The B-17G was one of the most heavily armed bombers of the war, fielding up to 13 12.7mm (0.50in) machine guns.

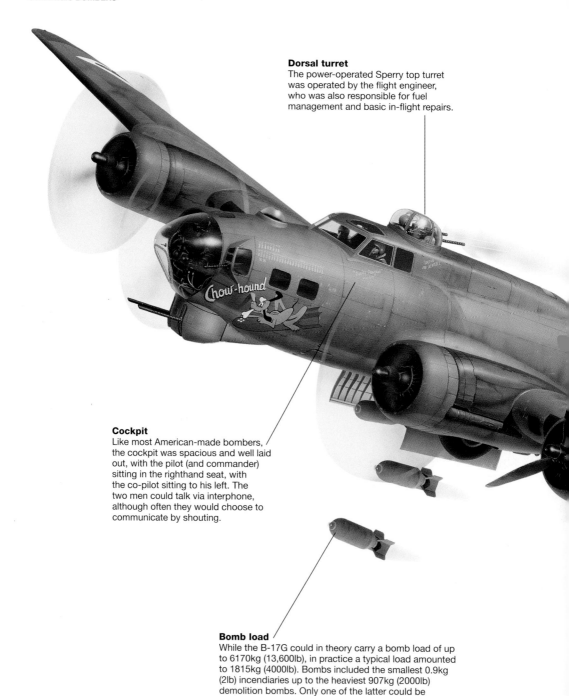

Dorsal turret
The power-operated Sperry top turret was operated by the flight engineer, who was also responsible for fuel management and basic in-flight repairs.

Cockpit
Like most American-made bombers, the cockpit was spacious and well laid out, with the pilot (and commander) sitting in the righthand seat, with the co-pilot sitting to his left. The two men could talk via interphone, although often they would choose to communicate by shouting.

Bomb load
While the B-17G could in theory carry a bomb load of up to 6170kg (13,600lb), in practice a typical load amounted to 1815kg (4000lb). Bombs included the smallest 0.9kg (2lb) incendiaries up to the heaviest 907kg (2000lb) demolition bombs. Only one of the latter could be carried, due to the dimensions of the bomb bay.

Boeing B-17G Flying Fortress

Assigned to the 322nd Bombardment Squadron of the
91st Bomb Group, 'Chow-hound' was a Boeing-built
B-17G that flew its first operational sortie in January
1944. It was destroyed by flak over Caen in August
1944, with the loss of all but one crew member.

Boeing B-17G

Weight (Maximum take-off): 29,700kg (65,500lb)

Dimensions: Length: 22.66m (74ft 4in), Wingspan:
32.60m (103ft 9in), Height: 5.82m (19ft 1in)

Powerplant: Four 895kW (1200hp) Wright R-1820-97
Cyclone radial nine-cylinder air-cooled piston engines

Maximum speed: 462km/h (287mph)

Range: 3219km (2000 miles)

Ceiling: 10,850m (35,600ft)

Crew: 10

Armament: One 12.7mm (0.5in) M2 Browning
machine guns flexibly mounted in both cheek
and waist positions and above radio operator's
compartment, two 12.7mm (0.5in) M2 Browning
machine guns in dorsal and ventral ball turrets and
two in tail position; up to 7,983kg (17,600lb) carried
both internally and externally

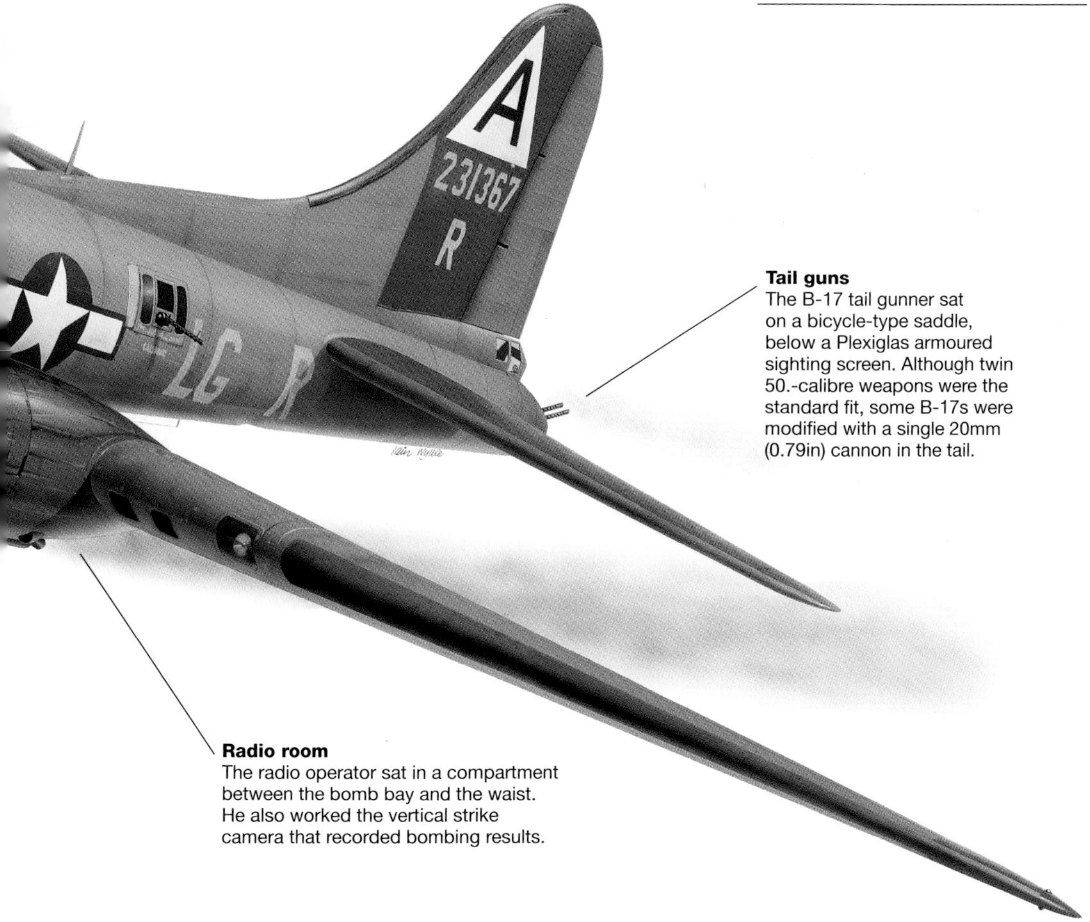

Tail guns
The B-17 tail gunner sat
on a bicycle-type saddle,
below a Plexiglas armoured
sighting screen. Although twin
50.-calibre weapons were the
standard fit, some B-17s were
modified with a single 20mm
(0.79in) cannon in the tail.

Radio room
The radio operator sat in a compartment
between the bomb bay and the waist.
He also worked the vertical strike
camera that recorded bombing results.

1944, the same load could be carried to the same target by the RAF's high-speed two-seat de Havilland Mosquito at a fraction of the cost, and with far greater safety.

By contrast, the BQ-9 'Aphrodite' modification packed a colossal punch. This was a B-17 converted to be a radio-controlled flying bomb, packed with 9100kg (20,000lb) of Torpex high explosive to be used against hardened targets such as U-boat pens. Fitted with an open cockpit, a two-man crew would fly the aircraft to height, then bail out, with the aircraft then flown on to the target by a controller in an accompanying B-17 mothership. Fifteen Aphrodite missions were attempted, but due to the inadequate nature of the remote-control equipment, none hit their targets, and the programme was abandoned. Other B-17 conversions saw the aircraft used as a long-range reconnaissance platform as the F-9, and four were converted into a transport designated the C-108. The first example of the C-108, derived from a B-17E, was fitted out as a VIP transport and used as a personal aircraft by General MacArthur.

Other users

Towards the end of the war, the US Navy also began to operate the B-17G, acquiring 48 examples designated the PB-1, for maritime patrol. These were later joined by 31 PB-1Ws, which were modified with extra fuel tanks to give the aircraft an endurance of around 22 hours. The PB-1Ws carried the one-megawatt AN/APS-20 Seasearch S-band radar in a fairing under the bomb bay to become the world's first operational Airborne Early Warning (AEW) aircraft.

Perhaps the most surprising wartime user of the B-17 was the Luftwaffe, with around 40 examples that had crash-landed in German-held territory returned to airworthy status. The special operations unit Kampfgeschwader 200 utilized several captured B-17s during the war on various clandestine missions, including long-range reconnaissance and the ferrying and resupply of agents in enemy territory, receiving the spurious designation Dornier Do 200 to hide its true origin.

Latter roles

Postwar, B-17s saw further service in many air forces worldwide. The last combat use occurred when Israeli Fortresses bombed Egyptian targets during the Suez Crisis of 1956. The B-17 was also utilized extensively as a civilian aircraft, seeing widespread use as an airliner and transport in the years immediately following the war. The aircraft also enjoyed enjoying a hugely successful secondary career in firefighting, with its fine handling qualities and immense strength rendering it particularly suitable as a water bomber.

As such, and somewhat ironically, an aircraft famous for starting fires all over the world spent the latter part of its career putting them out. The last B-17 firefighting missions were flown in 1985, bringing the operational career of this iconic aircraft to a close.

RAF SERVICE

As with earlier models, both the B-17F and B-17G were supplied to the RAF, which designated them the Fortress II and Fortress III respectively. Only 19 Fortress IIs entered British service, and all served with Coastal Command for the maritime patrol role, along with three of the 85 Fortress IIIs supplied to the RAF. Operating from the Azores, the north of Scotland and Northern Ireland, the reliability of the rugged Fortresses proved well suited to their remote bases.

Although not possessing a range capability as impressive as that of the B-24, the B-17s proved successful and were credited with sinking 11 U-boats in RAF service as well as performing mundane but demanding and essential work on meteorological flights over the Atlantic in all weathers. The Fortress III, however, was primarily used as an electronic warfare aircraft with 100 Group, Bomber Command, operating at night and carrying a wide variety of active electronic countermeasures to interfere with German radar and mount 'spoof' raids as decoys to genuine attacks.

Designated the Fortress Mk III (SD), these Fortresses carried Gee and LORAN radio navigation equipment as well as H2S navigation radar in a chin fairing replacing the under-nose turret. Monica tail-warning radar was carried, and the Fortress became the primary aircraft equipped with 'Jostle' aircraft – a VHF ECM device that blanketed the entire German ground-to-air radio band, rendering communication impossible. A large piece of equipment requiring 2000kW (2.68hp) of power to operate, Jostle necessitated the use of a large aircraft, and the Fortress proved ideal. Canada also received the Fortress during the war; No. 168 Heavy Transport Squadron RCAF used six B-17Es and B-17Fs to operate transatlantic mail flights between Ontario and Europe from late 1943 to December 1946.

Consolidated B-24 Liberator

Although never as famous as the Flying Fortress, the B-24 was an altogether more versatile machine, and in some respects more capable. More B-24s were built than any other US combat aircraft in history.

A later design than the B-17, the Liberator was conceived following a 1938 USAAC request asking for Consolidated to construct Flying Fortresses under licence. After company representatives visited Boeing's factory in Seattle, they decided instead to design a superior bomber of their own, which took shape as the Consolidated Model 32 under chief designer Isaac M. Laddon. This decision met with the approval of the Air Corps, and a formal specification was written around Consolidated's design in January 1939.

Rolled out in December, nearly five years after the Boeing aircraft first appeared, the XB-24 was an altogether more modern design, featuring a wing of unusually high aspect ratio designed by freelance aeronautical designer David R. Davis and tested on a Consolidated Coronado flying boat, delivering excellent cruise efficiency. The aircraft also featured a tricycle undercarriage; a first for an American heavy bomber.

More spacious

Other advanced features included its tambour-panel bomb bay doors, which operated in much the same fashion as a roll-top desk and created much less drag than conventional bomb doors, allowing for a higher speed in the bombing run. The bomb bay itself, split into two compartments, was notably more spacious than that of the B-17

The first major production Liberator variant was the B-24D, with the 0.9 metre (3ft) nose extension first seen on the RAF's Liberator Mk II.

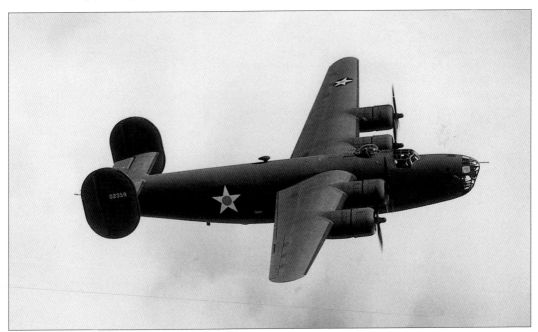

and could accommodate up to 7200kg (16,000lb) of bombs – although this amount was rarely used in practice, as to do so decreased both range and altitude performance. Designed and constructed to perform at an admirable speed, the Model 32 was flown for the first time on 29 December 1939.

The XB-24 design had already attracted the interest of foreign powers by this time, and orders were placed even before its first flight for 120 aircraft for France and 164 for the UK, on top of the 36 on order for the USAAC. Testing revealed the aircraft was deficient in speed, necessitating the switch from mechanically supercharged Pratt & Whitney R-1830 engines to turbo-supercharged units. The tail was also increased in span by 60cm (2ft). These changes resulted in the redesignation of the prototype as the XB-24B. A service test batch of seven YB-24s had already been ordered in April 1939.

Although neutral at the time, the US prioritized export orders over the supply of aircraft to the USAAC. As a result, the RAF were the first to take the B-24 into service, receiving six of the seven YB-24s after these were released for sale in November 1940 (now designated LB-30A). The RAF named the new aircraft the 'Liberator', a name that would later be officially adopted by the US.

The seventh YB-24 went into US air service and was redesignated as simply B-24, becoming the only B-24 with no suffix letter ever to exist. These first aircraft were not fitted with the turbo-supercharged engines or self-sealing fuel tanks that both the USAAC and RAF wanted, but as they did possess excellent range, they inaugurated the RAF's transatlantic Return Ferry Service, flying ferry pilots back to North America after they had made delivery flights to the UK. Next off the production line were 20 examples of the first production version Liberator Mk Is (designated LB-30B in the US). Built to British order, most of them would enter service

Consolidated B-24D (assembly ship)

Weight (Maximum take-off): 29,029kg (64,000lb)
Dimensions: Length: 20.22m (66ft 4In), Wingspan: 33.52m (110ft), Height: 5.46m (17ft 11in)
Powerplant: Four 895kW (1200hp) Pratt & Whitney R-1830-43 Twin Wasp 14-cylinder air-cooled radial piston engines
Maximum speed: 488km/h (303mph)
Range: 3700km (2300 miles)
Ceiling: 9876m (32,400ft)
Crew: 10
Armament: One 12.7mm (0.5in) Browning M2 machine gun flexibly mounted in nose, ventral tunnel; two 12.7mm (0.5in) Browning M2 machine guns mounted in tail turret

Consolidated B-24D Liberator

This B-24D-CO Liberator (41-23683), named 'Jo-Jo's Special Delivery', served with the 389th Bombardment Squadron, 93rd Bomb Group, Eighth Air Force. Painted with green and yellow diagonal stripes, it was deployed as a 'Green Dragon' assembly ship, whose role was to help get the large number of bombers flying into their formations safely and towards their intended target.

with 120 Squadron Coastal Command for maritime patrol, equipped with ASV radar and sometimes fitted with four 20mm (0.79in) cannon in a ventral pack. These were the first of many Liberators to serve in such a role on both sides of the Atlantic.

Following the Liberator Is were nine examples of the B-24A for the US, differing from the Liberator I only in their defensive armament. The majority of the B-24As were assigned to Transport Command, and in September 1941, two B-24As, marked with prominent flags of the still-neutral US, flew members of the Harriman mission from Washington to Moscow, the stage between Scotland and the USSR requiring a non-stop flight of 5070km (3150 miles).

New variants
By this time, the Liberator II (LB-30) had appeared, of which 165 would be built. This variant introduced a 78.7cm (31in) longer nose ahead of the cockpit and replaced several of the handheld machine guns with a British Boulton Paul four-gun turret in dorsal and tail positions. Considered the first combat-ready Liberator, these aircraft were built to British contract with British equipment, and no equivalent B-24

variant existed in US service, although 75 examples were requisitioned from British deliveries in response to the Pearl Harbor attack and fitted with a Martin turret in the dorsal position and handheld weapons elsewhere. These would be the first US Liberators to enter combat when three LB-30s of the 7th Bomber Group attacked a Japanese airfield in the Celebes on 17 January 1942. Liberator IIs were also the first to operate as heavy bombers in RAF service, operating with Middle East Command during the summer of 1942.

Meanwhile, a new variant combined the fuselage of the LB-30 with the wings and engines of the XB-24B fitted with turbo superchargers. This variant introduced the distinctive flattened oval shape cowlings, providing intakes for intercooler and supercharger, for the first time.

The B-24C also included a newly designed Consolidated hydraulic tail turret, but only nine examples were built before attention shifted to a further refined version, the B-24D, which was the first to be built in prodigious numbers: 2696 were built, 366 of which were supplied to Britain, where they were known as the Liberator III or IIIA depending on armament fit (or as the Liberator V when equipped with more fuel tanks). Except for its use of Buick-built R-1830-65 engines in place of the D model's R-1830-43s, the Ford-built B-24E was exactly the same, and 801 were built, with the majority being used as trainers.

The XB-24F was a solitary experimental aircraft fitted with an alternative de-icing system, and the B-24G was a B-24D built by North American Aviation, although all but the first 25 appeared with a Consolidated nose turret as fitted to

the B-24J. Most of the 430 B-24Js built saw action in the Mediterranean.

European theatre
The B-24D and its derivatives paved the way for Liberator operations in Europe, becoming the first USAAF heavy bombers to attack Europe when around a dozen aircraft bombed Ploiesti oil refinery in Romania on 12 June 1942. The first use of the B-24 by the Eighth Air Force followed on 9 October, when B-24D and Es of the 93rd BG raised Lille, and operations would gradually increase in number and strength over the next few years.

Initial B-24 losses were heavy, and like the B-17, the aircraft was found to be particularly vulnerable to head-on attack, leading to various extemporized gun mounts in the nose. The aircraft was generally not as popular with aircrew as the fortress as it was less resilient to battle damage, possessed a lower ceiling and was trickier to fly, especially at low speed.

The B-24 could fly further and faster than the B-17 and carry a greater bomb load. As a result, it was favoured by the Air Force General Staff. Eventually, the B-24 would become the most numerous US heavy bomber in Europe, making up around half of the Eighth Air Force and a much greater proportion of the other US Air Forces operating in the theatre.

Operation Tidal Wave
The most famous raid flown by early B-24s was Operation Tidal Wave, which saw 177 B-24s from Eighth and Ninth Air Force units fly from Libya to once again attack the oil refinery at Ploiesti, Romania. The mission, flown at low level, was a disaster, with only 88 of the attacking aircraft making it back to Libya (55 with battle damage). The damage inflicted on

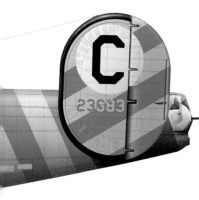

Consolidated B-24D Liberator

This B-24D, serial number 123599, was part of the 93rd Bomb Group,
Eighth Air Force.

Consolidated B-24D

Weight (Maximum take-off): 29,029kg (64,000lb)
Dimensions: Length: 20.22m (66ft 4in), Wingspan:
33.52m (110ft), Height: 5.46m (17ft 11in)
Powerplant: Four 895kW (1200hp) Pratt & Whitney
R-1830-43 Twin Wasp 14-cylinder air-cooled radial
piston engines
Maximum speed: 488km/h (303mph)
Range: 3700km (2300 miles)
Ceiling: 9876m (32,400ft)
Crew: 10
Armament: One 12.7mm (0.5in) Browning M2
machine gun flexibly mounted in nose, ventral tunnel,
and one in each of the left and right waist positions;
two 12.7mm (0.5in) Browning M2 machine guns
mounted in both top turret and tail turret; up to
5806kg (12,800lb) of bombs, normal offensive load
2268kg (5,000lb)

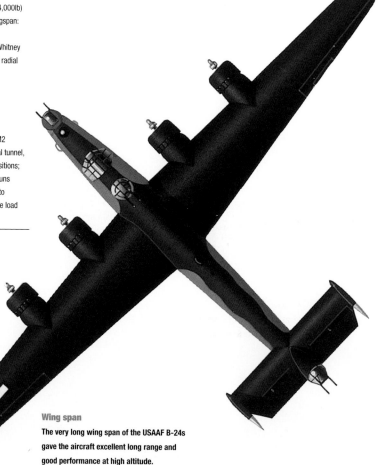

Wing span

The very long wing span of the USAAF B-24s
gave the aircraft excellent long range and
good performance at high altitude.

the refineries was repaired within weeks, and net oil production was actually greater than before the raid. In addition to the bombing, US crews claimed the destruction of 52 German and Romanian fighters; in fact, fighter losses amounted to eight.

Despite the generally desultory results of the raid, it was presented as a great success by US propaganda, aided by spectacular photographs and film taken during the attack. Five Medals of Honor were awarded, three posthumously; the most for any single air operation of the war.

Meanwhile, in the Pacific, the B-24 was in great demand, its greater range

and speed rendering it more suitable for the long-distance missions that prevailed there. The B-24 would remain the premier strategic bombing asset in the Pacific and CBI theatres until the advent of the B-29.

H and J models
The problem of vulnerability to frontal attack was addressed in the B-24H, which would be built in large numbers. This model adopted the Emerson A-15 electrically powered nose turret above the bomb-aiming position, giving the aircraft its classic profile. A total of 3100 B-24Hs rolled off the production line, mostly from Ford's Willow

Consolidated B-24H
Weight (Maximum take-off): 29,700kg (65,500lb)
Dimensions: Length: 20.62m (67ft 8in), Wingspan: 33.52m (110ft), Height: 5.48m (18ft)
Powerplant: Four 895kW (1200hp) Pratt & Whitney R-1830-43 Twin Wasp or R-1830-65 piston engines
Maximum speed: 466km/h (290mph)
Range: 3380km (2100 miles)
Ceiling: 8534m (28,000ft)
Crew: 10
Armament: Two 12.7mm (0.5in) Browning machine guns flexibly mounted in nose, upper, ventral, and tail turrets, one 12.7mm (0.5in) Browning machine gun flexibly mounted in each waist position; normal offensive bomb load was 2268kg (5,000lb)

Consolidated B-24H Liberator
B-24H-25-CF (serial no. 42-50383), called 'King Kong', flew with the 702nd Bombardment Squadron, 445th Bomb Group, Eighth Air Force. Pilot Robert D. Russell and his crew completed 10 missions aboard 'King Kong'. The aircraft was later lost on a mission over Kassel, Germany, on 27 September 1944.

Consolidated B-24H Liberator
B-24H-15-FO (serial no. 42-52728), nicknamed 'LIFE', was piloted by 2nd Lt. Volney W. Wiggins of the 813th Bombardment Squadron, 485th Bomb Group, Fifteenth Air Force.

Consolidated B-24H Liberator
This aircraft was part of the 726th Bombardment Squadron, 451st Bomb Group, Fifteenth Air Force, flying from various bases in Italy in 1944. 'The Stork' was piloted by Lt. Robert Blair.

Wings
The use of heavy box spars resulted in a stiff wing structure, allowing maximum space for fuel tanks.

Machine guns
The B-24H included 10 12.7mm (0.5in) Browning machine guns, installed in electrically actuated twin-gun nose, upper, ventral and tail turrents, and single gun waist positions on each side of the fuselage.

Bomb load
The B-24H's bomb load was carried vertically in racks. The unique roller-type bomb doors retracted upwards into the fuselage sides when opened, reducing drag.

Camouflage
This B-24 is painted in a standard olive drab upper surfaces and neutral grey undersides, the two colours demarcated along the lower fuselage by a wavy line.

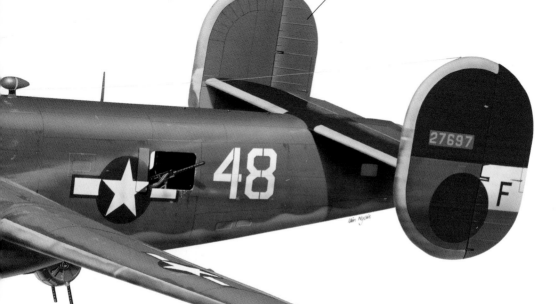

Belly turret
The underside turret fired a pair of 12.7mm (0.5in) machine guns from a powered turret.

Consolidated B-24H

Weight (Maximum take-off): 29,700kg (65,500lb)

Dimensions: Length: 20.62m (67ft 8in), Wingspan: 33.52m (110ft), Height: 5.48m (18ft)

Powerplant: Four 895kW (1200hp) Pratt & Whitney R-1830-43 Twin Wasp or R-1830-65 piston engines

Maximum speed: 466km/h (290mph)

Range: 3380km (2100 miles)

Ceiling: 8534m (28,000ft)

Crew: 10

Armament: Two 12.7mm (0.5in) Browning machine guns flexibly mounted in nose, upper, ventral, and tail turrets, one 12.7mm (0.5in) Browning machine gun flexibly mounted in each waist position; normal offensive bomb load was 2268kg (5,000lb)

Run assembly line. Other changes introduced with this model included staggered waist gun positions to allow greater freedom of movement for the gunners. These positions were also glazed with plexiglass for the first time, with improvements to both the dorsal and tail turrets for greater visibility. The H model was also supplied to the RAF as the Liberator VI, equipped with a British-made turret. The B-24J (Liberator VIII in RAF service), of which 6678 were built, was very similar to the H model but substituted a hydraulically powered Consolidated A-6 turret in place of the Emerson nose turrets due to shortages of the earlier turret.

The J model was the only B-24 variant to be built by all five companies producing B-24s: Consolidated, Ford, North American, Douglas and Bell. Of these, Ford's Willow Run plant was the largest. At its peak, Ford's plant was producing a Liberator every 59 minutes. Ford engineers also tinkered with the design, grafting a single fin and rudder tail design from a B-23 Dragon onto the rear fuselage of a B-24D to produce the B-24ST (ST standing for Single Tail). Results were promising enough that the aircraft was rebuilt with the tail from a C-54 transport and redesignated

the XB-24K. With handling greatly improved by the redesign, plans were laid to produce the B-24N in quantity, essentially a single-tailed B-24J with a spherical Emerson ball turret in the nose position; 5168 were ordered but production was abruptly cancelled at the end of hostilities, and only the XB-24N prototype and seven YB-24N service test aircraft were built.

The tail design did not disappear completely, however, as it was utilized on the Navy's PB4Y-2 Privateer – essentially a stretched Liberator optimized for low- and medium-altitude operations. Weight growth had become a concern by the time the B-24J was pouring off the assembly lines, and both the B-24L and B-24M were attempts to redress this tendency, with the ventral ball turret removed on the L (though reintroduced on the M) and a lightened tail turret. In most other respects, these two models – 4260 of which were built – were little changed from the J model. The vast quantities of these later-model Liberators saw the aircraft used extensively across the entire globe. In total, 18,188 B-24s would be built by the time production abruptly ceased in 1945.

Consolidated B-24J Liberator

This B-24J-100-CO Liberator (serial no. 42-100407), named 'Little Lambsy Divey', flew with the 755th Bombardment Squadron, 458th Bomb Group. The aircraft's name was inspired by the popular song "Mairzy Doats" (1943) by Jerry Livingston.

Consolidated B-24J

Weight (Maximum take-off): 32,295kg (71,200lb)
Dimensions: Length: 20.47 m (67ft 2in), Wingspan: 33.52m (110ft), Height: 5.48m (18ft)
Powerplant: Four 895kW (1200hp) Pratt & Whitney R-1830-35 Twin Wasp, R-1830-41 or R-1830-65 14-cylinder air-cooled radial piston engines
Maximum speed: 483km/h (300mph)
Range: 2480km (1540 miles)
Ceiling: 8534m (28,000ft)
Crew: 10
Armament: Two 12.7mm (0.5in) Browning machine guns flexibly mounted in nose, upper, ventral and tail turrets, one 12.7mm (0.5in) Browning machine gun flexibly mounted in each waist position; maximum short-range bomb load of 5806kg (12,800lb); normal offensive bomb load was 2268kg (5,000lb)

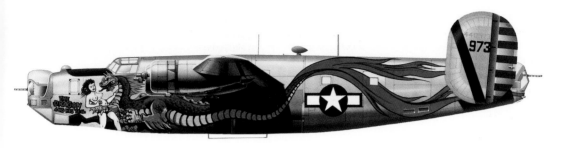

Consolidated B-24J Liberator

This famous B-24J (serial number 44-0973), nicknamed 'The Dragon and His Tail', was part of the 43rd Bomb Group. It has since been restored to mint condition by the Collings Foundation of Stow, MA.

Although designed as a heavy bomber, the Liberator's roomy fuselage, impressive carrying capacity and great range saw it perform a variety of other roles. As with the B-17, a gunship variant was designed, the XB-41, with greater defensive armament, but only one was built after tests showed its performance was too poor to warrant further development.

The B-24 was also utilized as a remotely controlled bomb as the BQ-8 but exploded prematurely in mid-air for unknown reasons, killing the two-man crew (one of whom was Joseph P. Kennedy, brother of John F. Kennedy). Far more successful was the aircraft's use as an anti-submarine maritime patrol aircraft.

The RAF had employed the Liberator, designated the GR Mk I, for this work even before the US entered the war as the aircraft was able to close the 'Mid-Atlantic Gap' beyond the range of any other RAF Coastal Command aircraft in which U-boats had previously operated with impunity.

For over a year, only 120 Squadron of Coastal Command was equipped with Liberators and provided the sole air cover for convoys in the Mid-Atlantic Gap. The Very Long Range (VLR) Liberators carried extra fuel tanks in the bomb bay and dispensed with some armour and armament to give them the necessary range but were equipped with both ASV radar and the powerful Leigh Light to allow attacks by both day and night.

Vital naval role

Later B-24Ds, B-24Gs and Hs and B-24Js would be converted for RAF and RCAF anti-submarine use as the GR Mk V, GR Mk VI and GR Mk VIII respectively. Adopting the same aircraft for the same role, the US Navy received 976 navalized B-24D, J, L and Ms, designating all of them the PB4Y-1. By mid-1943, Liberators ranged east from Iceland, Scotland, Northern Ireland and the Azores and west from Nova Scotia, Greenland, the Caribbean, Panama and even Ascension Island, abruptly and decisively turning the fight against the U-boats in the Allies' favour. The Liberator was the most successful anti-submarine aircraft of the war, accounting for a total of 93 U-boats sunk, either exclusively or in concert with other aircraft or ships. It played a decisive role in the Allied victory in the Battle of the Atlantic.

The RAF never employed the Liberator as a heavy bomber in Western Europe, but 20 Liberator VIs were utilized by a squadron in 100 Group to carry electronic jamming equipment to counter German radar while flying with the bomber stream. In the USAAF, the 36th Bombardment Squadron was the Eighth Air Force's only electronic warfare squadron and used specially equipped B-24s to jam German VHF communications during daylight raids. The British primarily used their Liberator bomber variants against the Japanese, operating with South East Asia Command from bases in India.

Transport model

The CBI theatre also saw the Liberator widely used as a transport aircraft by US forces, and this would form a significant role for the aircraft, with the

Consolidated B-24J

Weight (Maximum take-off): 32,295kg (71,200lb)

Dimensions: Length: 20.47m (67ft 2in), Wingspan: 33.52m (110ft), Height: 5.48m (18ft)

Powerplant: Four 895kW (1200hp) Pratt & Whitney R-1830-35 Twin Wasp, R-1830-41 or R-1830-65 14-cylinder air-cooled radial piston engines

Maximum speed: 483km/h (300mph)

Range: 2480km (1540 miles)

Ceiling: 8534m (28,000ft)

Crew: 10

Armament: Two 12.7mm (0.5in) Browning machine guns flexibly mounted in nose, upper, ventral and tail turrets, one 12.7mm (0.5in) Browning machine gun flexibly mounted in each waist position; maximum short-range bomb load of 5806kg (12,800lb); normal offensive bomb load was 2268kg (5,000lb)

C-87 'Liberator Express' transport variant being both converted from existing B-24D airframes and built from scratch at Consolidated's Fort Worth plant. The Liberator was a better transport than most converted bombers and was able to carry between 20 and 25 passengers or up to 5400kg (12,000lb) of cargo. However, the aircraft still suffered from some drawbacks as a result of its original role, not least an oversensitivity to centre of gravity changes – never a problem with bombs, which are heavy but small and fixed at one point.

As a bomber, the aircraft was never expected to land with its bomb load still on board, and its undercarriage was not designed for landing with the sort of weight the C-87 was regularly carrying. As a result, undercarriage failures, particularly of the nose gear, were commonplace. Nonetheless, when the USAAF began supplying war material from India to China over 'the Hump' (as the dangerous route over the Himalayas was nicknamed), the C-87 was the only readily available American transport aircraft with sufficient high-altitude

performance to fly this route carrying a meaningful cargo load. Although supplemented by C-54 Skymasters and C-46 Commandos – altogether better transport aircraft with much better flying characteristics – the C-87 was never entirely supplanted.

Earlier Liberator variants had been used with considerable success as airliners by BOAC and QANTAS and as transports by the RAF. The most famous example of all was a Liberator II, named 'Commando', converted to become the personal transport of Winston Churchill. In 1944, Commando's fuselage was stretched, and it was given a single fin and rudder. Churchill regularly took the controls of this aircraft in flight, but he was far from the only famous Liberator pilot. Oscar-winning actor Jimmy Stewart flew around 40 combat missions as commander of the B-24-equipped 703rd Bombardment Squadron of the Eighth Air Force.

Operation Carpetbagger

In an offshoot of the transport role, several suitably modified B-24Ds were

utilized from August 1943 onwards on clandestine missions in a combined venture of the USAAF and the Office of Strategic Services (OSS). Codenamed 'Operation Carpetbagger', the crews flew Liberators in support of various resistance (and other) underground groups across occupied Europe. Painted in overall gloss black, as this finish was found to be the least conspicuous if caught in a searchlight beam, the Liberators flew spies and commando groups into and out of Europe and also retrieved over 5000 shot-down aircrew. Due to the

---

Consolidated B-24M Liberator

Weight (Maximum take-off): 32,295kg (71,200lb)
Dimensions: Length: 20.47m (67ft 2in), Wingspan: 33.5m (110ft), Height: 5.48m (18ft)
Powerplant: Four Pratt & Whitney R-1830-35 Twin Wasp, R-1830-41 or R-1830-65 14-cylinder air-cooled radial piston engines
Maximum speed: 483km/h (300mph)
Range: 2480km (1540 miles)
Ceiling: 8534m (28,000ft)
Crew: 10
Armament: Two 12.7mm (0.5in) Browning machine guns flexibly mounted in nose, upper, ventral ball and tail turrets, one 12.7mm (0.5in) Browning machine gun flexibly mounted in each waist position. Maximum short-range bomb load of 5806kg (12,800lb), normal offensive bomb load was 2268kg (5,000lb)

Consolidated B-24M Liberator
This B-24M-25-CO (serial no. 44-42251) was nicknamed 'Slower than Rotation' and flew with the 436th Bombardment Squadron, 7th Bomb Group, Eighth Air Force.

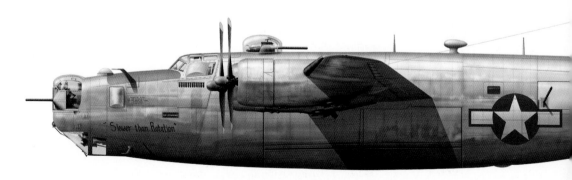

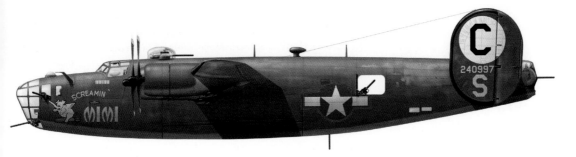

Consolidated B-24D Liberator

B-24D-120-CO (serial no. 42-40997), nicknamed 'Screamin' Mimi', served with the 565th Bombardment Squadron, 389th Bomb Group, Eighth Air Force. In February 1944, it was modified to drop supplies to Resistance groups as part of Operation Carpetbagger. During an operation, it hit a hill near the drop zone, crashed, and caught fire at St-Cyr-de-Valorges, in the Loire Department, France.

Consolidated B-24D

Weight (Maximum take-off): 29,029kg (64,000lb)
Dimensions: Length: 20.22m (66ft 4in), Wingspan: 33.52m (110ft), Height: 5.46m (17ft 11in)
Powerplant: Four 895kW (1200hp) Pratt & Whitney R-1830-43 Twin Wasp 14-cylinder air-cooled radial piston engines
Maximum speed: 488km/h (303mph)
Range: 3700km (2300 miles)
Ceiling: 9876m (32,400ft)
Crew: 10
Armament: One 12.7mm (0.5in) Browning M2 machine gun flexibly mounted in nose, ventral tunnel, and one in each of the left and right waist positions; two 12.7mm (0.5in) Browning M2 machine guns mounted in both top turret and tail turret (later production B-24Ds were fitted with further machine guns); up to 5806kg (12,800lb) of bombs, normal offensive load 2268kg (5,000lb)

dangerous, low-altitude nighttime flying required, crews were selected initially from anti-submarine units who had received training in low-level flying and highly accurate navigation. Later, these crews and the Carpetbagger B-24s were used to supply General Patton's Third Army with fuel after it outran its supply line, delivering 3,114,264L (822,791 US gal) of 80 octane gasoline to three airfields in Belgium and France.

Usage by other nations

In addition to the widespread use of the Liberator by US and British forces, the aircraft was also used by the South African Air Force (SAAF). Two SAAF squadrons based in Italy flew the type, operating relief flights in support of the uprisings in Warsaw and Krakow in addition to regular bombing sorties.

Australia, too, received Liberators in 1944, at the suggestion of USAAF General George Kenney, commander of Allied Air Forces in the Southwest Pacific Area. Seven RAAF squadrons, an operational training unit and two 'Special Duties' flights had been equipped with the aircraft by the end of World War II in August 1945. Flying mainly from bases in the Northern Territory, Queensland and Western Australia, Australian B-24s conducted bombing raids against Japanese targets in New Guinea, Borneo and the Netherlands East Indies whilst the Special Duties flights supported covert operations. A total of 287 B-24s of various models were supplied to the RAAF, remaining in service until 1948.

An altogether more unexpected operator of the B-24 was the Soviet Union, who were very interested in the aircraft, primarily due to its prodigious range. Only one Liberator was supplied to the USSR through lend-lease

channels. However, 73 B-24s that had crash-landed on Soviet territory in various states of repair were used to make around 30 airworthy examples, some of which may have been operational before the end of the war. These aircraft were retained in Soviet service until at least 1949.

The Luftwaffe also used three captured Liberators on clandestine missions with KG 200. One of these was shot down by German anti-aircraft fire on 6 April 1945.

B-24J Liberator

CUTAWAY KEY

1 Rudder trim tab
2 Fabric-covered rudder
3 Rudder hinges (metal leading edge)
4 Starboard tailfin
5 Leading-edge de-icing boot
6 Starboard rudder horn
7 Rudder push-pull tube
8 Rear navigation light
9 Tailplane stringers
10 Consolidated (or Motor Products) two-gun electrically-operated tail turret (0.5 in/12.7mm)
11 Elevator torque tube
12 Elevator trim tab
13 Elevator frame (fabric-covered)
14 Rudder trim tab
15 Tab control linkage
16 Rudder post
17 Light alloy rudder frame
18 HF aerial
19 Tailfin construction
20 Metal-covered fixed surfaces
21 Tailplane front spar
22 Port elevator push/pull tube
23 Elevator drive quadrant
24 Elevator servo unit
25 Rudder servo unit
26 Ammunition feed track (tail turret)
27 Fuselage aft main frame
28 Walkway
29 Signal cartridges
30 Longitudinal 'Z' section stringers
31 Control cables
32 Fuselage intermediate secondary frames
33 Ammunition box

34 Aft fuselage camera installation
35 Lower windows
36 Waist gun support mounting
37 Starboard manually operated waist gun (0.5 in / 12.7 mm)
38 Waist position (open)
39 Wind deflector plate
40 Waist position hinged cover
41 Port manually-operated 'waist' gun (0.5in/12.7mm)
42 Dorsal aerial
43 Ball-turret stanchion support beam
44 Ammunition box
45 Ball-turret stanchion
46 Midships window
47 Turret well
48 Cabin floor
49 Tail-bumper operating jack
50 Tailbumper fairing
51 Briggs-Sperry two-gun electrically-operated ball-turret (0.5in/12.7mm)
52 Turret actuation mechanism
53 Bomb-door actuation sprocket (hydraulically-operated)
54 Bomb-door corrugated inner skin
55 Bomb-bay catwalk (box keel)
56 Bomb-bay catwalk vertical channel support members (bomb release solenoids)
57 Bomb-door actuation track and rollers
58 Wing rear spar
59 Bomb-bay access tunnel
60 Fuselage main frame/bulkhead
61 D/F loop housing
62 Whip antenna
63 Oxygen cylinders
64 Aileron cable drum

65 Starboard flap extension cable
66 Wing rib cut-outs
67 Wing centre section carry-through
68 Two 5-man inflatable dinghies
69 Flap hydraulic jack
70 Flap/cable attachments
71 Hydraulically-operated Fowler flap
72 Wing rear spar
73 Port mainwheel well and rear fairing
74 Engine supercharger waste gate
75 Three auxiliary self-sealing fuel cells (port and starboard)
76 Wing outer section
77 Aileron gear boxes
78 Flush riveted smooth metal wing skinning
79 Port statically-balanced aileron (fabric-covered)
80 Port wingtip
81 Port navigation light
82 Wing leading-edge de-icing boot
83 Hopper-type self- sealing oil tank (125 litres/32.9 US gal)
84 Engine nacelle
85 895kW (1200hp) Pratt & Whitney Twin Wasp R-1830-65 14-cylinder two-row radial engine
86 Hamilton Standard Hydromatic constant-speed airscrew (3.53m/11ft 7in diameter)
87 Landing/taxiing light
88 Nacelle structure
89 Supercharger ducting
90 12 self-sealing inter-rib fuel cells (wing centre section)
91 Martin two-gun electrically-operated dorsal turret (0.5in/12.7mm)
92 Turret mechanism
93 Fuselage main frame/bulkhead
94 Radio compartment starboard window

95 Bomb-bay catwalk access trap
96 Radio-operator's position
97 Sound-insulation wall padding
98 Emergency escape hatch
99 Pilot's seat
100 Co-pilot's seat
101 Co-pilot's rudder pedals
102 Instrument panel
103 Windscreen panels
104 Compass housing
105 Control wheel
106 Control wheel mounting
107 Control linkage chain
108 Fuselage forward main frame bulkhead
109 Pitot heads
110 Navigator's chart table
111 Navigator's compartment starboard window
112 Chart table lighting
113 Astro-dome
114 Consolidated (or Emerson) two-gun electrically-operated nose turret (0.5in/12.7mm)
115 Turret seating
116 Optically-flat bomb-aiming panel
117 Nose side-glazing
118 Bombardier's prone couch
119 Ammunition boxes
120 Navigator's swivel seat
121 Navigator's compartment entry hatch (via nosewheel well)
122 Nosewheel well
123 Nosewheel door
124 Forward-retracting free-swivelling nosewheel (self-aligning)
125 Mudguard
126 Torque links
127 Nosewheel oleo strut
128 Angled bulkhead

129 Cockpit floor support structure
130 Nosewheel retraction jack
131 Smooth-stressed Alclad fuselage skinning
132 Underfloor electrics bay
133 Roll top desk-type bomb-bay doors (four)
134 Supercharger nacelle cheek intakes
135 Ventral aerial (beneath bomb-bay catwalk)
136 Nacelle/wing attachment cut-out
137 Wing front spar nacelle support
138 Undercarriage front-pivoting shaft
139 Drag strut
140 Bendix scissors
141 Internal bomb load (max 3629kg /8,000lb)
142 Starboard mainwheel
143 Engine-mounting ring
144 Firewall
145 Monocoque oil tank
146 Mainwheel oleo (Bendix pneudraulic strut)
147 Side brace (jointed)
148 Undercarriage actuating cylinder
149 Starboard mainwheel well and rear fairing
150 Fowler flap structure
151 Wing front spar
152 Wing leading-edge de-icing boot
153 All-metal wing structure
154 Spanwise wing stringers
155 Aileron trim tab (starboard only)
156 Wing rear spar
157 Wing ribs (pressed and built-up former)
158 Statically-balanced aileron (metal frame)
159 Starboard navigation light
160 Wingtip structure

SPECIFICATION B-24J LIBERATOR

Crew

Up to 10.

Powerplant

Four Pratt & Whitney R-1830-65 14-cylinder air-cooled radial engines with General Electric B-22 exhaust-driven turbo-chargers, each delivering 895kW (1200hp) at take-off and maintaining this power at a military rating up to 9692m (31,800ft).

Performance:

Maximum speed at 30,000ft: 483km/h (300mph); Initial climb rate: 312.42m (1025ft) per minute; Service ceiling: 8534m (28,000ft)

Weights

Empty: 17,236kg (38,000lb); Combat: 25,401kg (56,000lb); Maximum overload: 32,295kg (71,200lb); Maximum bombload: 5806kg (12,800lb)

Dimensions

Length: 20.47m (67ft 2in); Height: 5.48m (18ft); Wing span: 33.52m (110ft); Wing area: 319.4m^2 (1048 sq ft)

Armament

Ten 12.7mm (0.5in) Browning machine guns in nose, upper, ventral, ball and tail turrets and in waist positions, with a total of 4,716 rounds. Maximum short-range bomb load was 5806kg (12,800lb), while normal offensive load was 2268kg (5,000lb).

A Boeing B-24J Liberator, armed with an internal bomb load of 3629kg (8,000lbs).

Boeing B-29 Superfortress

The product of the most expensive single arms programme of the war, the B-29 was, by a considerable margin, the most advanced bomber to see service during the conflict. It remains the only aircraft to have used a nuclear weapon in anger.

Work on what would become the B-29 began at Boeing in 1938 due to the realization that the B-17 did not have sufficient range to effectively prosecute a potential war in the Pacific theatre. Although the Air Corps initially lacked sufficient funds to develop the design, and production of such an aircraft at that time was prohibited by the Secretary of War, Boeing continued work on the aircraft by the company as a private venture. The situation changed after famed aviator Charles Lindbergh publicly called for increased production of US bombers to counter the threat from Germany and General Henry 'Hap' Arnold, Chief of the Air Corps, encouraged Research and Development efforts to go ahead.

Challenging build

In December 1939, the Air Corps issued a challenging specification for a so-called 'superbomber' that could deliver 9100kg (20,000lb) of bombs to a target 4292km (2667 miles) away and at a speed of 640km/h (400mph).

Boeing was well placed to respond to this specification with the design it had been working on, internally designated the Model 345, but designs were also submitted by Consolidated, Lockheed and Douglas. Lockheed and Douglas would abandon the project, but Consolidated persisted, and their design would eventually see wartime service (only just in time) as the B-32 Dominator.

A contract was issued for two prototypes of the Model 345 (one for static testing only) on 24 August 1940. Designated the XB-29 by the Air Corps, a third prototype was added to the order in December. During May 1941, a further order was placed for 14 service test aircraft and 250 production B-29s, a figure that was increased to 500 in January 1942, demonstrating the great importance that was being placed on the new design.

The XB-29 was a highly advanced aircraft that pioneered the use of pressurization and remotely controlled defensive armament controlled by an electromechanical computer system. These features were wedded to an untried powerplant, the Wright R-3350 Duplex-Cyclone, which promised high power output but was suffering from teething issues when the B-29 design was being finalized and would prove the most troublesome aspect of the design when it entered service.

Boeing B-29

Weight (Maximum take-off): 61,000kg (135,000lb)

Dimensions: Length: 30.18m (99ft), Wingspan: 43.05m (141ft 3in), Height: 8.46m (27ft 9in)

Powerplant: Four 1600kW (2200hp) Wright R-3350-23 Duplex-Cyclone 18-cylinder air-cooled radial piston engines

Maximum speed: 575km/h (357mph)

Range: 5230km (3250 miles)

Ceiling: 9710m (31,850ft)

Crew: 11

Armament: Two 12.7mm (0.5in) Browning M2/AN machine guns in each of four remotely controlled turrets, one 20mm (0.79in) M2 cannon and two 12.7mm (0.5in) Browning M2/AN machine guns in rear turret; up to 9071kg (20,000lb) bomb load

---

Boeing B-29 Superfortress

Named 'The Cannuck', this B-29 flew with the 500th Bomber Group, 73rd Bomber Wing. The ten 12.7mm (0.5in) Browning M2/AN machine guns in remote-controlled turrets and two tail machine guns are apparent on this artwork.

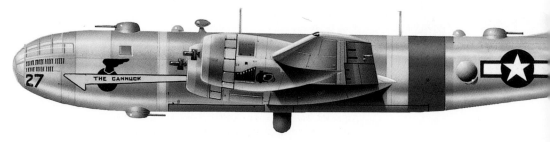

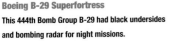

Boeing B-29 Superfortress
This 444th Bomb Group B-29 had black undersides
and bombing radar for night missions.

Battle of Kansas

If building the prototype Superfortress was a difficult endeavour, the effort required to mass-produce such a complicated aircraft was immense, resulting in the use of four main assembly factories, though there were thousands of subcontractors involved in the project. Nonetheless, a little over a year after the contract was placed, the first prototype was rolled out and made its first flight on 21 September 1942 from Boeing's Everett Field in Seattle. Initial testing was impeded by engine problems. The first flight of the second prototype on 30 December 1942, for example, was curtailed by an engine fire. Tragically, the same aircraft

experienced a major engine fire shortly after take-off on 18 February 1943 and crashed into a factory, killing all 10 on board as well as 20 workers in the building.

Despite this setback, work continued apace to get the aircraft into production and service as soon as possible, and the urgency with which the programme went ahead led to serious problems, as shortcuts were made in the production process. The B-29 also entered production while necessary changes were still being made to the design, leading to a farcical situation in which aircraft were being delivered off the production line direct to modification centres for extensive rebuilds to incorporate the latest changes, resulting in a serious bottleneck. Changes required included the replacement of defective seals around the gun-sighting blisters, the replacement of distorted cockpit glazing, the replacement of substandard cannon plugs (of which there were over half a million in total in the completed aircraft) and the strengthening of the wing's internal structure. The most serious change, however, was to the Wright engines. Each R-3350 was removed and disassembled, then rebuilt with added baffles to accelerate the airflow over the cylinders, new exhaust valves with improved metallurgy, new rocker

arms (drilled with holes to allow better oil flow) and modified nose casings and engine sumps (also to improve oil flow).

By the end of 1943, although over 100 aircraft had been built, only 15 were airworthy, with the rest awaiting modification, a situation made worse by the fact that most of the work had to take place in the open as the B-29 was too large to fit inside most existing hangars. In a huge effort, driven by General Arnold and subsequently nicknamed the 'Battle of Kansas', specialist USAAF technicians were called in from all over the US, and 600 workers were transferred from the B-29 assembly lines. Frequently working in sub-zero temperatures, the 1200 technicians assigned to the Wichita factory and the Modification Centers managed to complete the modifications in five weeks.

First mission

With the worst of the production problems ironed out, the B-29's first operational mission was flown on 5 June 1944, when over 70 aircraft flew from Indian bases and bombed the marshalling yard at Bangkok. Five aircraft were lost, though none from enemy action.

Further raids occurred at a fairly slow pace, with mainland Japan bombed for the first time since the Doolittle raid of 1942 on 15 June, when

Boeing B-29 Superfortress

Nicknamed 'Dina Might', this aircraft
was assigned to the 421st Bombardment
Squadron, 504th Bombardment Group. Piloted
by James L. Hardison, on 23 May 1945 'Dina
Might' took off from North Field on Tinian
Island on a night bombing mission against
Tokyo. On returning, it crash-landed and was
destroyed. The crew survived unhurt.

Guns
The pressurized fuselage demanded the
use of remote-controlled gun barbettes,
provided in the form of four twin-gun
turrets located above and below the
fuselage, and one in the tail.

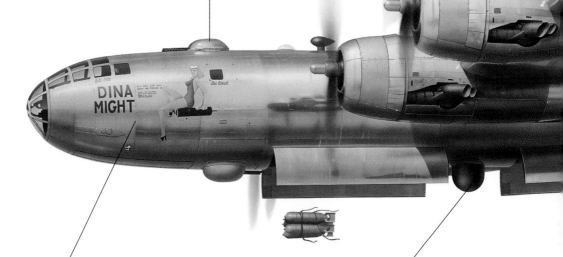

Crew
The crew of 11 consisted of pilot, co-pilot,
bombardier, flight engineer, navigator, radio
operator, radar observer, right gunner, left
gunner, central fire control and tail gunner.

Radar
The AN/APQ-13 bombing radar was located
between the twin bomb bays. The radome
housed a 0.76m (30in) rotating dish antenna.
radar navigator, signaller, central fire
controller and two gunners. The rear turret
was usually unmanned.

Colour scheme
Although early B-29s flew painted
with olive drab over neutral grey
camouflage, most served unpainted
to reduce weight.

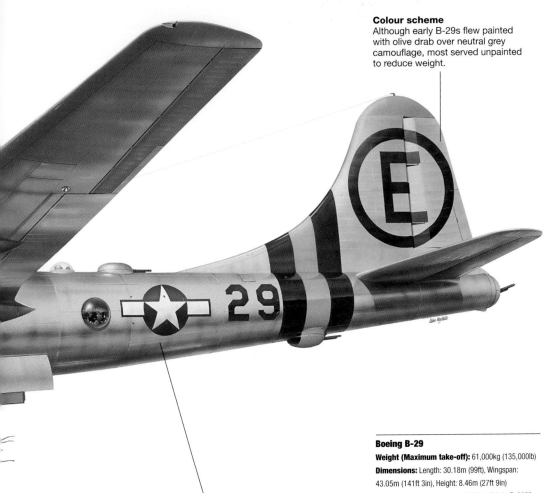

Rear fuselage
A pressurized compartment was found
between the rear of the bomb bay
and the start of the dorsal fin. This
contained the gunners' positions as
well as crew rest bunks.

Boeing B-29

Weight (Maximum take-off): 61,000kg (135,000lb)

Dimensions: Length: 30.18m (99ft), Wingspan:
43.05m (141ft 3in), Height: 8.46m (27ft 9in)

Powerplant: Four 1600kW (2200hp) Wright R-3350-
23 Duplex-Cyclone 18-cylinder air-cooled radial piston
engines

Maximum speed: 575km/h (357mph)

Range: 5230km (3250 miles)

Ceiling: 9710m (31,850ft)

Crew: 11

Armament: Two 12.7mm (0.5in) Browning M2/AN
machine guns in each of four remotely controlled
turrets, one 20mm (0.79in) M2 cannon and two
12.7mm (0.5in) Browning M2/AN machine guns in rear
turret; up to 9071kg (20,000lb) bomb load

The B-29s' first combat missions were flown from India to targets in Burma, raids on Japan from bases in China beginning shortly afterwards. In this dramatic photograph, B-29s of the 468th Bomb Group, 20th Air Force, unload over a Japanese supply depot close to Mingaladon airfield near Rangoon.

75 Superfortresses attacked the iron and steelworks at Yawata from forward bases in China. Though this raid was militarily insignificant, and only one bomb actually hit the intended target, causing relatively little damage, it heralded the start of the most effective strategic bombing campaign in history.

The early B-29 raids saw many aircraft fall victim to mechanical failures, and engine fires were still worryingly commonplace, even following the modifications made to the R-3350 engines. On the other hand, the Superfortress demonstrated that its high speed and operating altitude would prove extremely difficult for the Japanese to combat, either with anti-aircraft guns or interceptor aircraft.

New island bases

B-29 operations were given a major boost following the invasion and capture of Saipan, Tinian and Guam in the Mariana Islands. Only part of Japan was within range of Superfortresses operating from Chinese bases, and these presented logistical difficulties, as fuel and equipment had to be flown over 'the Hump' from India. Chinese bases were also within range of Japanese bombers.

By contrast, the island bases of the Marianas were beyond the range of Japanese aircraft, could be easily resupplied by ship and allowed the B-29 to attack targets at any point on the Japanese mainland. Construction of US bases commenced even before the end of hostilities on the islands, and

the first Superfortress raid, against the major Japanese naval base at Truk Atoll, was flown from Saipan on 28 October 1944.

The first attack against a target in Japan followed in November, when 111 B-29s bombed Tokyo. Attacks would be flown at a regular pace for the rest of the war and attained a new level of destructiveness when a switch to lower-level incendiary raids was made in February 1945, the first target being Kobe. The horrific culmination of this effort came on the night of 9/10 March 1945, when 279 B-29s firebombed Tokyo in the single deadliest raid of the war (including the later atomic bombing of Hiroshima and Nagasaki).

Approximately a quarter of the city was destroyed and between 90,000–100,000 people were killed,

virtually all of them civilians, with over a million more made homeless. Twelve B-29s were lost to anti-aircraft fire. Raids continued until the end of the war, including further attacks on Tokyo, with the last in May. Ultimately, half the city would be destroyed and over four million people made homeless. The switch to lower-altitude operation for the incendiary raids saw the introduction of a new variant, the B-29B, with all armament but the tail guns removed and an APQ-7 'Eagle' bombing-through-overcast radar fitted in an airfoil-shaped radome under the fuselage. All 311 B-29Bs were built by the Bell plant at Marietta, Georgia.

A new kind of warfare

By far the most famous missions in the history of the B-29, however, were the nuclear attacks on Hiroshima and

Nagasaki. The B-29 was the only aircraft in the US inventory able to carry the large and heavy 'Fat Man' plutonium implosion bomb or the smaller (but still very large) 'Little Boy' uranium-gun bomb but required modification to do so. Use of the British Avro Lancaster was seriously considered as it possessed a very large bomb bay and would have required less

extensive modification, but there was considerable political pressure to utilize an American design. Aircraft adapted to carry the nuclear weapons were codenamed 'Silverplate', and a total of 46 would be built during the war.

The aircraft featured a modified bomb bay to allow for the large size of both atomic bomb designs and were fitted with a British Type G single-

Boeing B-29

Weight (Maximum take-off): 61,000kg (135,000lb)
Dimensions: Length: 30.18m (99ft), Wingspan: 43.05m (141ft 3in), Height: 8.46m (27ft 9in)
Powerplant: Four 1600kW (2200hp) Wright R-3350-23 Duplex-Cyclone 18-cylinder air-cooled radial piston engines
Maximum speed: 575km/h (357mph)
Range: 5230km (3250 miles)
Ceiling: 9710m (31,850ft)
Crew: 11
Armament: Two 12.7mm (0.5in) Browning M2/AN machine guns in each of four remotely controlled turrets, one 20mm (0.79in) M2 cannon and two 12.7mm (0.5in) Browning M2/AN machine guns in rear turret; up to 9071kg (20,000lb) bomb load

Boeing B-29 Superfortress

'The Big Stick' was a typical Superfortress of the 73rd Bomb Wing – the first unit to assemble in the Marianas and comprising the 497th, 498th, 499th and 500th Bombardment Squadrons. A 500th Bombardment Squadron aircraft, 'The Big Stick' was based on Saipan in 1945.

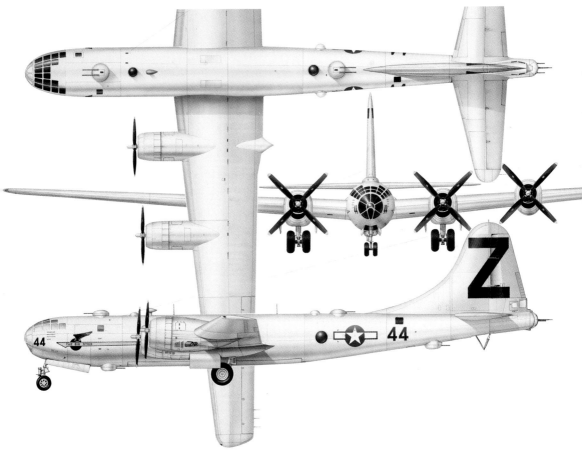

Boeing B-29 Superfortress

CUTAWAY KEY

1 Temperature probe
2 Nose glazing
3 Optically-flat bomb-aiming panel
4 Bombsight
5 Windscreen panels
6 Forward gun sight
7 Bombardier's seat
8 Pilot's instrument console
9 Control column
10 Co-pilot's seat
11 Pilot's seat
12 Side console panel
13 Cockpit heating duct
14 Nose undercarriage leg strut
15 Steering control
16 Twin nosewheels
17 Retraction struts
18 Nosewheel doors
19 Underfloor control cable runs
20 Pilot's back armour
21 Flight engineer's station
22 Forward upper gun turret, four 12.7mm (0.5in) machine-guns, 500 rpg
23 Radio operator's station
24 Chart table
25 Navigator's instrument rack
26 Fire extinguisher bottle
27 Forward lower gun turret, two 12.7mm (0.5in) machine-guns, 500 rpg
28 Ventral aerial
29 Navigator's seat
30 Hydraulic system servicing point
31 Access ladder
32 Forward cabin rear pressure bulkhead
33 Armoured bulkhead

34 Pressurised tunnel connecting front and rear cabins
35 Astrodome observation hatch
36 Forward bomb racks
37 Bomb-hoisting winches
38 Catwalk
39 Bomb rack mounting beam
40 Pressurised tunnel internal crawlway
41 D/F loop aerial
42 Radio communications aerials
43 Starboard main undercarriage wheel bay
44 Wing inboard fuel tanks 5356 litres (1415 US gal)
45 Starboard inner-engine nacelle
46 Intercooler exhaust flap
47 Engine-cooling air outlet flaps
48 Engine cowling panels
49 Hamilton Standard four-bladed, constant-speed propellers, 5.05m (16ft 7in) diameter
50 Propeller hub pitch change mechanism
51 Starboard outer engine nacelle
52 Exhaust stub
53 Wing outboard fuel tanks, 4991 litres (1320 US gal), maximum internal fuel load 35,443 litres (9,363 US gal) including bomb bay ferry tanks
54 Wing bottom skin stringers
55 Leading-edge de-icing boots
56 Starboard navigation light
57 Fabric-covered aileron
58 Aileron tab
59 Flap guide rails
60 Starboard Fowler-type flap
61 Flap rib construction
62 Inboard nacelle tail fairing

63 Life raft stowage
64 Wing panel centreline joint
65 Wing/fuselage attachment mainframes
66 Pressurisation ducting
67 Heat exchanger
68 Centre-section fuel tank, 1,333 US gal (5046 litres)
69 Cabin heater
70 Pressurisation control valve
71 Fuselage framing
72 Rear bomb bay, four 9C7kg (2000lb) bombs shown
73 Bomb rack
74 Access door
75 Rear cabin front pressure bulkhead
76 Radio aerial mast
77 Upper gun turret sighting hatch
78 Upper gunner's seat
79 Remote gun controller
80 Radio and electronics racks
81 Upper gun turret, two 12.7mm (0.5in) machine-guns, 500 rpg
82 Rear pressure bulkhead
83 Finroot fillet
84 Starboard tailplane
85 Starboard elevator
86 Leading-edge de-icing boot
87 Tailfin construction
88 HF aerial cable
89 Fintip fairing
90 Fabric-covered rudder construction
91 Rudder tab
92 Pressurised tail gunner's compartment
93 Armoured-glass window panels

94 Tail gun camera
95 20mm (0.79) cannon, 100 rounds
96 Twin 12.7mm (0.5in) machine-guns, 500 rpg
97 Remotely-controlled ball turret
98 Elevator tab
99 Port fabric-covered elevator construction
100 Tailplane leading-edge de-icing boot
101 Tailplane construction
102 Fin/tailplane attachment joints
103 Tail turret ammunition boxes
104 Retractable tail bumper
105 Oxygen bottles
106 APU fuel tank
107 Rear ventral turret, two 12.7mm (0.5in) machine-guns, 500 rpg
108 Auxiliary power unit (APU)
109 Oblique camera
110 Vertical camera
111 Crew entry door
112 Batteries
113 Pressure bulkhead access door
114 Crew rest bunks
115 Toilet
116 Radio communications tuning units
117 Remote gun sight
118 Gun aiming blister
119 Gunner's seat, port and starboard
120 Voltage regulator
121 Bomb door hydraulic jacks
122 Rear bomb bay doors
123 Port Fowler flap
124 Flap shroud ribs
125 Rear spar

126 Outer wing panel joint
127 Aileron tab
128 Fabric-covered aileron construction
129 Wingtip fairing
130 Port navigation light
131 Wing stringers
132 Outer wing panel ribs
133 Front spar
134 Leading-edge nose ribs
135 Leading-edge de-icing boots
136 Port wing fuel tank bays
137 Engine nacelle firewall
138 Nacelle construction
139 Engine mounting frame
140 Twin mainwheels
141 Main undercarriage leg strut
142 Mainwheel leg pivot mounting
143 Port mainwheel bay
144 Hydraulic retraction jack
145 Nacelle tail fairing
146 Self-sealing oil tank, 322 litres (85 US gal)
147 Hydraulic reservoir
148 Mainwheel doors
149 Exhaust stub
150 Exhaust-driven turbo-supercharger
151 Intercooler
152 Engine-cooling air exit flaps
153 Exhaust collector ring
154 Wright Cyclone R-3350-23 18-cylinder, two-row radial engine
155 Engine intake ducting
156 Forward bomb bay doors
157 Twenty 227kg (500lb) bombs, maximum bombload 9072kg (20,000lbs)

The B-29 Superfortress could carry a bombload of more than 9000kg (20,000lbs), the largest bombload of any aircraft in World War II.

SPECIFICATION BOEING B-29 SUPERFORTRESS

Type

11 (Pilot, Co-pilot, Bombardier, Flight Engineer, Navigator, Radio Operator, Radar Observer, Right Gunner, Left Gunner, Central Fire Control, Tail Gunner)

Powerplant

Four 1641kW (2200hp) Wright R-3350-23 Cyclone 18 turbocharged radial piston engines

Performance

Maximum speed at 7620m (25,000ft): 576km/h (358mph); Cruising speed: 370km/h (230mph); Service ceiling: 9710m (31,850ft); Range: 5230km (3,250 miles)

Weights

Empty: 31,815kg (70,140lb); Maximum take off: 56,245kg (124,000lb)

Dimensions

Length: 30.18m (99ft); Height: 9.02m (29ft 7in); Wingspan: 43.05m (141ft 3in); Wing area: 161.27m² (1736 sq ft)

Armament

Two 12.7mm (0.5in) guns each in four remotely-controlled, power-operated turrets, and three 12.7mm (0.5in) guns or two 12.7mm (0.5in) guns and one 20mm (0.79in) cannon in the tail turret; plus a bombload of up to 9072kg (20,000lb) of incendiaries, conventional munitions or nuclear weapons

Boeing B-29 Superfortress

Named after the mother of the pilot, Colonel Paul Tibbets, B-29 'Enola Gay' dropped the first atomic bomb, codenamed 'Little Boy', which destroyed three-quarters of the city of Hiroshima on 6 August 1945.

point bomb attachment and release gear, which had been developed for the 5443kg (12,000lb) 'Tallboy' bomb. Weight was reduced by dispensing with all turrets and armament apart from the rear guns.

Later Silverplate aircraft received reversible-pitch propellers to reduce landing run and used more powerful Wright R-3350-41 engines with direct fuel injection that were also more powerful than the engines of standard B-29s. The aircraft also introduced a station for a new crew member called the 'weaponeer', whose job was to monitor the release and detonation of the bomb.

Atomic nemesis

A new era in warfare began when a Silverplate B-29 – named 'Enola Gay' after the mother of the pilot, Paul Tibbetts – dropped the first 'Little Boy' weapon over Hiroshima on 6 August 1945. Enola Gay was accompanied by two other Silverplate aircraft to record the effects of the weapon. The bomb exploded 580m (1900ft) above the city and immediately killed over 60,000 people (exact numbers are unknown but may be as high as 140,000), while 69 per cent of the buildings in the city were destroyed. The second atomic bomb attack occurred on 9 August 1945, when the B-29 'Bockscar' commanded by Charles Sweeney dropped the

considerably more powerful 'Fat Man' weapon on Nagasaki. Casualties, though still enormous, were fewer than at Hiroshima due to the city's position in a narrow valley, which confined the bomb's immediate effects. Within a week, the Japanese surrender declaration had been broadcast, bringing World War II to an end.

Postwar service

The B-29 enjoyed a long career in the frontline after World War II. The Silverplate B-29s remained the only nuclear-capable USAAF aircraft for some time after the war, and the standard B-29 would see combat service once again as a conventional heavy bomber during the Korean War.

Both the RAF and RAAF would operate 91 and two B-29s respectively in the postwar era, but the Soviet Union reverse-engineered the Superfortress after interning four examples that had made emergency landings in Soviet territory (in accordance with the USSR's neutrality in the Pacific at the time) and put the aircraft into production as the Tu-4, receiving the NATO codename 'Bull'. A total of 847 Tu-4s was built, and in 1951, a Tu-4 was used to test-drop the RDS-3 atomic bomb. Bizarrely, the Superfortress thus became the first aircraft to drop a nuclear weapon for both sides in the Cold War.

An improved B-29 with more powerful Pratt & Whitney R-4360

Boeing B-29 (Silverplate)

Weight (Maximum take-off): 61,000kg (135,000lb)
Dimensions: Length: 30.18m (99ft), Wingspan: 43.05m (141ft 3in), Height: 8.46m (27ft 9in)
Powerplant: Four 1640kW (2200hp) Wright R-3350-41 Duplex-Cyclone 18-cylinder air-cooled radial piston engines
Maximum speed: 587km/h (365mph)
Range: 5230km (3250 miles)
Ceiling: 10,240m (33,600ft)
Crew: 12
Armament: Two 12.7mm (0.5in) Browning M2/AN machine guns in rear turret; up to 9071kg (20,000lb) bomb load

engines, a beefed-up structure and a taller fin and rudder entered production in 1947, designated the B-50 Superfortress (originally B-29D), and 350 were built. One of these was used as the mothership for the Bell X-1 rocket aircraft: the first aircraft to break the sound barrier. The B-50 was subsequently used as a basis for the development of the highly successful C-97 Stratofreighter cargo aircraft, KC-97 tanker and Boeing 377 Stratocruiser airliner. After the bombing role had passed to later designs, Superfortresses were used for a wide range of secondary duties, such as air-sea rescue, electronic intelligence gathering and air-to-air refuelling. The last of the Superfortresses in US service was the WB-50 weather reconnaissance variant, which was retired in 1965.

Consolidated B-32 Dominator

Conceived as a backup to the B-29, the B-32 suffered delays due to numerous teething issues. This, coupled with the success of the Superfortress, resulted in the Dominator entering only limited service during 1945.

In June 1940, the USAAC approached Consolidated with a request to build a similar design to the B-29 some two years after work had begun at Boeing. The Consolidated Model 33 took shape as a larger development of the successful B-24, featuring a high aspect ratio Davis wing with similar twin tails but with a larger, more streamlined fuselage.

Originally designed to feature both cabin pressurization and remotely controlled defensive armament, the prototype XB-32 made its first flight on 7 September 1942, two weeks before the B-29 first took to the air.

Philippines and Japan

Unfortunately, the XB-32 soon ran into difficulties. The pressurization system never functioned properly and was abandoned. Similarly, the remote gun turrets, sighted by a Sperry analogue computer, were subject to severe problems and replaced with conventional manned gun turrets.

Stability problems saw the twin tails replaced by an enormous single fin and rudder. By the end of 1944, only five production aircraft had been built, but by May 1945, sufficient numbers were available to allow the first combat mission to take place in the Philippines.

A few more bombing missions were flown before the B-32s switched to the photographic reconnaissance role, continuing beyond VJ Day as the Allies sought to gain more information about Japanese mainland facilities in preparation for occupation. During these missions, a B-32 became involved in the last aerial combat of World War II, when on 18 August 1945, it was engaged by 17 Japanese fighters over Tokyo in the mistaken belief that it was taking part in a bombing attack. Although neither side lost any aircraft, one of the B-32's crew was fatally wounded and became the last US casualty of World War II.

Consolidated B-32A Dominator
Weight (Maximum take-off): 55,905kg (123,250lb)
Dimensions: Length: 25.02m (82ft 1in), Wingspan: 41.15m (135ft), Height: 9.8m (32ft 2in)
Powerplant: Four 1600kW (2200hp) Wright R-3350-23A Duplex Cyclone eighteen-cylinder air-cooled radial piston engines
Maximum speed: 575km/h (375mph)
Range: 6100km (3800 miles)
Ceiling: 9400m (30,700ft)
Crew: 10
Armament: Two 12.7mm (0.5in) Browning M2 machine guns each in nose, tail, ventral and two dorsal turrets; up to 9072kg (20,000lb) bomb load

Consolidated B-32A Dominator
This B-32A (serial no. 42-108532) was part of 386th Bombardment Squadron and served in the Pacific theatre. Named 'Hobo Queen II', this aircraft was one of those involved in the final aerial combat of the war, when three N1K2-J Shiden-Kai fighters attacked the aircraft, but without causing any significant damage.

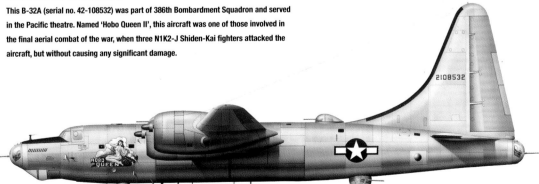

TACTICAL BOMBERS

While neglected in the interwar period due to the Air Corps' fixation on strategic bombing, tactical aircraft remained an important element of USAAC planning. Given that it was a branch of the Army, it is perhaps unsurprising that many types were developed with the primary purpose of supporting American ground forces in the field. The versatility of such designs also saw them being widely used by other nations. The following aircraft are featured in this chapter:

- Curtiss A-12 Shrike
- Martin B-10
- Martin 167 Maryland
- Martin 187 Baltimore
- Vultee A-31/A-35 Vengeance
- Douglas A-20 Havoc
- Douglas A-26 Invader
- North American B-25 Mitchell
- Martin B-26 Marauder

Two of the Doolittle Raid's 16 B-25B bombers, parked on the flight deck of USS *Hornet* (CV-8), 18 April 1942. The plane at right has tail # 40-2282. It is mission plane # 4, piloted by 2nd Lt. Everett W. Holstrom, Jr.

Curtiss A-12 Shrike

A radical aircraft in its day, the Shrike was essentially obsolete by the time World War II began but lingered on in service during the opening months of 1942.

With its colourful paint schemes and massive wheel spats, the Shrike was the absolute epitome of a mid-1930s Air Corps aircraft. Based on the earlier A-8 (confusingly also named the Shrike), of which only 13 were ever built, the A-12 replaced the liquid-cooled Curtiss Conqueror engine with a Wright Cyclone radial enclosed by a drag-reducing Townend ring after a single A-8 was tested with a Pratt & Whitney Hornet radial. This conversion was designated the YA-10. Although slower than the liquid-cooled aircraft, the radial engine was more reliable, simpler to maintain and – lacking a vulnerable cooling system – was perceived to be less susceptible to failure due to combat damage. The decision was made therefore to complete the remaining A-8s on order as the A-12 with radial engines.

Innovative monoplane

The A-8 had earlier caused a sensation by becoming the first monoplane production combat aircraft to enter

Curtiss A-12 Shrike

A Curtiss A-12 Shrike awaiting delivery to the Chinese Nationalist Air Force in 1936.

service in April 1932 with the Air Corps, the Boeing P-26 monoplane fighter only entering service eight months later, rendering virtually all the biplane bombers and fighters obsolete overnight. By the time the A-12 appeared, it wasn't quite such a sensational machine.

Nonetheless, it was still in the vanguard of military aviation progress. Only 46 would be built, and the first entered service during 1933 with the 3rd Attack Group, subsequently being used by the 8th and 18th Pursuit Groups. Nine USAAF A-12s were still in service at Hickam Field, Hawaii when Pearl Harbor was attacked but escaped damage. The surviving A-12s were grounded early in 1942.

Twenty A-12s were also supplied to China, and these would be the only examples to see combat, being used in the Second Sino-Japanese War, which

Curtiss A-12 Shrike

Weight (Maximum take-off): 2611kg (5756lb)
Dimensions: Length 9.83m (32ft 3in), Wingspan 13.41m (44ft), Height 2.74m (13ft)
Powerplant: One 510kW (690hp) Wright R-1820-21 Cyclone nine cylinder air-cooled radial piston engine
Maximum speed: 285km/h (177mph)
Range: 840km (520 miles)
Ceiling: 4620m (15,150ft)
Crew: 2
Armament: Four 7.62mm (0.3in) M1919 Browning machine guns fixed forward-firing in wheel fairings, one 7.62mm (0.3in) machine gun flexibly mounted in observer's cockpit; up to 220kg (485lb) bomb load

commenced in 1937 and merged into World War II. Although utilized as ground attack machines, on one occasion a group of 13 Aichi D1A1 biplane dive bombers happened across a flight of Chinese Shrikes and a dogfight ensued: two D1A1s were shot down by the Chinese A-12s without loss, with a third badly damaged. The few Chinese A-12s that survived until 1941 were reassigned to training duties.

Martin B-10

A revolutionary aircraft when it first appeared, the B-10 was reaching the end of its operational career when called upon to engage in combat missions during World War II.

When it first flew in February 1932, the private venture Martin Model 123 caused a sensation as it featured an all-metal monoplane airframe, enclosed cockpits, a rotating gun turret, retractable landing gear, an internal bomb bay and NACA engine cowlings. Martin received that year's Collier Trophy for building the XB-10 (as the model 123 was designated by the Army), and it set a precedent for bomber aircraft that would only be superseded by the advent of the jet engine. Despite its historical importance, being a peacetime design, comparatively few B-10s or any of its derivatives would be built.

Deliveries to Air Corps units began in July 1935, and 166 would be built for US use, though the relentless pace of aviation development meant the B-10 was obsolete by 1939, and the last few in USAAF hands were withdrawn during 1940. Martin was permitted to export the design in 1936, and orders were received from Argentina, Turkey, Siam (which became Thailand in 1939), China and the Netherlands.

Martin B-10

This early model Martin B-10 (serial no. 33-146) was written off after a landing accident at Bolling Field, Washington, D.C., in March 1935.

Service with other countries

Argentinian and Turkish aircraft saw no combat, but the B-10 was sent into action by three other nations, the first being China, which used its Model 139WCs against the Japanese during the Second Sino-Japanese War from 1937 onwards, including daring unescorted leaflet dropping raids over mainland Japanese cities in 1938. During the brief Franco-Thai war, Thai aircraft were used to bomb Vichy French targets in December 1940 and January 1941.

However, Netherlands East Indies (NEI) aircraft saw the greatest amount of combat. With 121 aircraft delivered, the NEI was the biggest export customer, flying both the Model 139WH and the improved Model 166, which featured uprated engines, a long 'greenhouse' canopy and redesigned

Martin B-10

Weight (Maximum take-off): 7439kg (16,400lb)
Dimensions: Length 13.64m (44ft 9in), Wingspan 21.49m (70ft 6in), Height 4.7m (15ft 5in)
Powerplant: Two 578kW (775hp) Wright R-1820-33 Cyclone nine cylinder air-cooled radial piston engines
Maximum speed: 343km/h (213mph)
Range: 2000km (1240 miles)
Ceiling: 7400m (24,200ft)
Crew: 3
Armament: One 7.62mm (0.3in) Browning M1919 machine guns flexibly mounted in nose, ventral and dorsal positions; up to 1025kg (2260lb) of bombs

wings. The NEI Martins were used to combat the Japanese invasion both in the Dutch East Indies and in Singapore. Six Martins were lost during sorties against Japanese shipping and other targets before the aircraft were withdrawn to Java in mid-January 1942.

Martin 167 Maryland

After losing out to Douglas to supply a new light bomber for the US Army Air Corps, Martin found a ready market for its speedy Model 167 overseas.

The first export customer for Martin's light bomber was France, which ordered 200 of the Model 167F, which differed from the prototype XA-22 (tested by the US) in its use of the Wright R-1820 Cyclone rather than the R-1830 Twin Wasp as well as French instrumentation and equipment. The imposition of an arms embargo saw the delivery delayed, but eventually, the Glenn Martin 167 A-3, as it was officially known by the French, entered service in early 1940.

During the German assault on France, the four squadrons equipped with 'Glenns' proved effective, the aircraft possessing relatively high speed and excellent manoeuvrability. Losses were markedly lower than similar types. Following the armistice, surviving French Martins were transferred to North Africa, where some were used to bomb British and Commonwealth forces.

Re-engined

The remaining 75 aircraft on the French order were taken on by Britain, which named the aircraft Maryland Mk I and re-engined the aircraft with Pratt & Whitney Twin Wasps. The aircraft proved suitably effective for the British to order a further 150 Maryland Mk IIs featuring two-speed superchargers.

RAF service

In RAF use, most Marylands saw action in North Africa and the Middle East, being mainly utilized in the photo reconnaissance role due to their higher speed than the Bristol Blenheim, which was the RAF's standard reconnaissance platform at the time. A Maryland supplied detailed information on the ships in Taranto Harbour in a daring low-level reconnaissance flight in very poor weather.

Combat role

The Maryland also proved surprisingly capable in aerial combat: ace reconnaissance pilot Adrian Warburton scored five confirmed 'kills' with the Maryland's fixed forward-firing guns. Only 450 Marylands were built as, by the middle of 1941, Martin had developed the improved Model 187 Baltimore.

Maryland I

Weight (Maximum take-off): 7624kg (16,809lb)
Dimensions: Length 14.2m (45ft 8in), Wingspan 18.7m (61ft 4in), Height 5m (16ft 3in)
Powerplant: Two 783kW (1050hp) Pratt & Whitney R-1830-S1C3-G Twin Wasp 14 cylinder air cooled radial piston engines
Maximum speed: 489km/h (304mph)
Range: 2100km (1300 miles)
Ceiling: 8991m (29,500ft)
Crew: 3
Armament: Four 7.7mm (0.303in) Browning Mk II machine guns fixed forward-firing in outer wings, one 7.7mm (0.303in) Vickers K machine gun in dorsal and ventral positions; up to 907kg (2,000lb) of bombs

Martin Maryland Mk I

This Martin Maryland Mk I was part of No. 431 Flight, RAF, and was based in Malta. The main role of No. 431 Flight was maritime reconnaissance, which played a crucial role in the success of the Battle of Taranto on 11 November 1940.

Martin 187 Baltimore

An enlarged and improved design derived from the Maryland, the Baltimore, like its predecessor, was not operated by the USAAF but saw sustained wartime use with other nations.

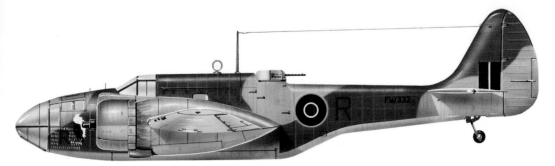

This Baltimore Mk V flew with No. 232 Wing, RAF, in the Mediterranean theatre in 1944. The unit was part of the Desert Air Force (DAF) from January 1944, made up of 18, 114 (Bostons) and 223 (Baltimores) Squadrons.

Baltimore V

Weight (Maximum take-off): 23,001lb (10,433kg)
Dimensions: Length 14.8m (48ft 6in), Wingspan 18.7m (61ft 4in), Height 4.32m (14ft 2in)
Powerplant: Two 1268kW (1700hp) Wright GR-2600-A5B 14-cylinder air-cooled radial piston engines
Maximum speed: 488km/h (305mph)
Range: 1577km (980 miles)
Ceiling: 7315m (24,000ft)
Crew: 3
Armament: Four 12.7mm M2 Browning machine guns fixed forward-firing in wings, two or four 7.7mm (0.303in) Browning machine guns in dorsal turret, two 7.7mm (0.303in) Browning machine guns flexibly mounted in machine guns in ventral position, provision for up to four fixed rearward firing 7.7mm (0.303in) machine guns on fuselage sides; up to 910kg (2000lb) of bombs

The Martin 167 Maryland had proved effective in service but suffered from overly cramped accommodation for the crew, so Martin developed the Model 187 with a deeper fuselage and more powerful engines for French use. Four hundred were ordered for the Armée de l'Air. Too late to see action with the French, the order was instead taken on by the RAF, who named the aircraft Baltimore Mk I. Later variants differed little from the Mk I, with improvements to the firepower and engines being made over the course of the aircraft's production life.

Cramped ride

Used exclusively in the Middle East and North Africa, the Baltimore represented a huge improvement over the Bristol Blenheim and was praised for its heavy armament, strength, manoeuvrability, bombing accuracy and relatively high performance. However,

despite the enlarged fuselage, it was still considered a cramped aircraft. Committed initially to low-level attacks without fighter escort against advancing Axis forces in the Western Desert, losses were heavy, but when operating at medium level, the Baltimore enjoyed a very low loss rate, with greater attrition resulting from non-combat causes than enemy action.

'Stormo Baltimore'

Other users received Baltimores passed on from RAF stocks, notably the Free French and Italian Co-belligerent Air Force, as well as Greece, Australia, South Africa and neutral Turkey. The Italians were particularly enthusiastic operators, naming one of their squadrons the 'Stormo Baltimore' in honour of the type.

As well as bombing, the Baltimore was utilized as reconnaissance aircraft, nocturnal intruder, target tug, high-

speed transport and maritime patrol, proving quite successful in the latter role, with eight U-boats credited as sunk. Most Baltimores were quickly retired after the war, though a few persisted in RAF service in Kenya until 1948, with the last Italian aircraft being withdrawn in the same year.

Vultee A-31/A-35 Vengeance

Although little known today, the Vengeance saw considerable action with Allied air forces in Burma, India and New Guinea, and proved to be a highly accurate dive bomber.

Like several of the operational aircraft produced in the US during World War II, the Vengeance owed its existence to the requirements of a foreign power – in this case, France. Vultee developed the V-72 as a private venture to meet a specification issued by the Armée de l'Air. France duly ordered 300 examples of the aircraft but fell to Germany before the order was delivered. Subsequently, in July 1940, the United Kingdom ordered 200 V-72s, naming the aircraft the 'Vengeance'.

Maiden flight

Flying for the first time on 30 March 1941, the V-72 was a large single-engine aircraft with an unusual W-plan wing design. The wing was set at a neutral angle of incidence to maximize dive performance, and this led to the aircraft assuming a pronounced nose-up attitude in level flight, restricting pilot view. After Pearl Harbor, the US commandeered 243 examples of the Vengeance, designating it the A-31.

By the time the V-72 was available, British operational doctrine was profoundly opposed to dive-bombing, and squadrons equipped with the Vengeance would not be used in action in Europe or the Mediterranean. Instead, British and Indian units used the Vengeance during intense fighting on the India/Burma frontier during 1943 and 1944. Australia utilized the Vengeance in New Guinea and in the Netherlands East Indies, achieving considerable success before the aircraft was replaced by more versatile fighter-bombers.

US units of the Tenth Air Force briefly operated the A-31 in combat in China, but most of the USAAF's A-31s were used as target tugs and trainers, as was the improved A-35, which introduced four degrees of wing incidence to improve the flying qualities of the Vengeance. Sixty-seven assigned to the Free French were likewise only used for training.

The final user was Brazil, which received 33 A-31s in 1943, flying them on anti-submarine patrols. The last Brazilian Vengeance was retired in 1948.

Vultee A-31 Vengeance III

Weight (Maximum take-off): 6486kg (14,300lb)

Dimensions: Length 12.12m (39ft 9in) Wingspan 14.63m (48ft), Height 4.67m (15ft 4in)

Powerplant: One 1193kW (1600hp) Wright R-2600-19 Twin Cyclone 14-cylinder air-cooled radial piston engine

Maximum speed: 443km/h (275mph)

Range: 2253km (1400 miles)

Ceiling: 6860m (22,500ft)

Crew: 2

Armament: Four 7.62mm (0.3in) Browning machine guns fixed forward-firing in wings, two 7.62mm (0.3in) Browning machine guns flexibly mounted in rear cockpit; up to 460kg of bombs in bomb bay, 220kg (500lb) bomb on wing racks

---

Vultee A-31 Vengeance III

A Vengeance Mark III (serial no. FB922), from No. 1583 Calibration Flight, South East Asia Command (SEAC) based at Chittagong, India.

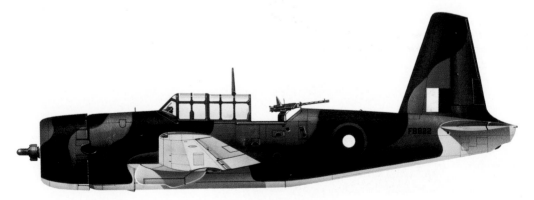

Douglas A-20 Havoc

Despite initial indifference from the USAAC, the fast and agile A-20 proved to be an exceptional attack bomber and saw widespread service in the air arms of many nations.

Development of the A-20 began in 1936 when Donald Douglas, Jack Northrop and Ed Heinemann met with USAAC personnel at Wright Field to draw up requirements for a light attack bomber. This resulted in the Northrop Model 7A design (Northrop then being a subsidiary of Douglas) intended to be powered by two 336kW (450hp) engines, to carry a 454kg (1000lb) bomb load and to be capable of a maximum speed of 402km/h (250mph).

Obsolescence and redesign

Even before the Model 7A was completed, analysis of combat in the Spanish Civil War indicated that the aircraft was already obsolescent. This, combined with the issuing of an Army requirement for a twin-engine bomber able to carry 544kg (1200lb) of bombs for 1931km (1200 miles) at 322km/h (200mph), saw the design reworked with a pair of 820kW (1100hp) Pratt & Whitney R-1830 S3C3-G Twin Wasp engines and various other changes, creating the Model 7B. By the time prototype construction was underway,

Jack Northrop had parted ways with Douglas, and the project became the Douglas Model 7B, with Ed Heinemann as chief designer. Built at Douglas's own expense, the Model 7B made its first flight on 26 October 1938 and immediately proved to have excellent handling and performance.

The only significant alteration made to the basic design was to move the horizontal tail surfaces forward slightly and to give them a slight dihedral. As a premonition of design changes to come, the aircraft featured an interchangeable nose: either a transparent 'bomber' nose with a bombardier's position and bombsight or a solid 'attack' nose fitted with six 7.62mm (0.3in) and two 12.7mm (0.5in) machine guns.

The Model 7B was in direct competition with designs from North American, Martin and Stearman, and though the Douglas aircraft won the contest, developments of both the Martin and North American designs would also be built in quantity as the Model 167 and B-25 respectively.

French order

The Model 7B had attracted the interest of the French Purchasing Commission even before flight testing was completed, and French representatives were invited to participate in the test flying programme. The flying career of the first prototype was brief, however, as it crashed on 23 January 1939, killing test pilot John Cable when his

---

Douglas A-20B

Weight (Maximum take-off): 10,795kg (23,800lb)
Dimensions: Length 14.63m (48ft), Wingspan 18.69m (61ft 4in), Height 5.51m (18ft 1in)
Powerplant: Two 1194kW (1600hp) Wright R-2600-11 Twin Cyclone 14-cylinder air-cooled radial piston engines
Maximum speed: 563km/h (350mph)
Range: 1328km (825 miles)
Ceiling: 8717m (28,600ft)
Crew: 3
Armament: Two 12.7mm (0.5in) Browning M2 machine guns fixed forward-firing on each side of forward fuselage, one 12.7mm (0.5in) flexible machine gun in the top gunner's position, one 7.62mm (0.3in) Browning M1919 machine gun flexibly mounted in ventral tunnel position; 1089kg (2400lb) bomb load

---

Douglas A-20B

An A-20B (41-3241) from the 47th Bomb Group, based at Souk-el-Arba, Tunisia, 1943. The aircraft is painted in a 'Desert Pink' finish, an effect of sunlight on the paint's pigmentation.

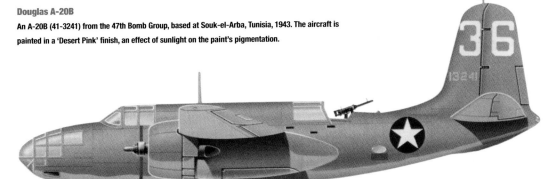

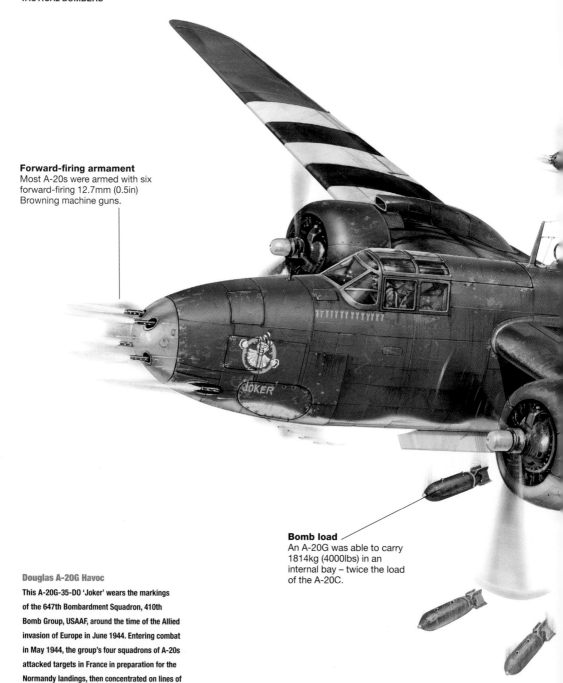

Forward-firing armament
Most A-20s were armed with six
forward-firing 12.7mm (0.5in)
Browning machine guns.

Bomb load
An A-20G was able to carry
1814kg (4000lbs) in an
internal bay – twice the load
of the A-20C.

Douglas A-20G Havoc

This A-20G-35-DO 'Joker' wears the markings
of the 647th Bombardment Squadron, 410th
Bomb Group, USAAF, around the time of the Allied
invasion of Europe in June 1944. Entering combat
in May 1944, the group's four squadrons of A-20s
attacked targets in France in preparation for the
Normandy landings, then concentrated on lines of
communication after D-Day.

Dorsal turret
The A-20G included a pair of flexible 7.62mm (0.3in) machine guns in the open dorsal position.

Douglas A-20G
Weight (Maximum take-off): 13,608kg (30,000lb)
Dimensions: Length 14.63m (48ft), Wingspan 18.69m (61ft 4in), Height 5.51m (18ft 1in)
Powerplant: Two 1194kW (1600hp) Wright R-2600-23 Twin Cyclone 14-cylinder air-cooled radial piston engines
Maximum speed: 523km/h (325mph)
Range: 1521km (945 miles)
Ceiling: 7200m (23,700ft)
Crew: 3
Armament: Six 12.7mm (0.5in) Browning M2 machine guns fixed forward-firing in nose, two 12.7mm (0.5in) Browning M2 machine guns in dorsal turret, one 12.7mm (0.5in) Browning M2 machine gun, flexibly in ventral position mounted behind bomb bay: up to 900kg (2000lb) of bomb load in bomb bay plus up to 910kg (2000lb) on underwing hardpoints

Ventral armament
The A-20 included a single 7.62mm (0.3in) machine gun on the underside of the fuselage, operated remotely.

Colours and markings
This A-20G is finished in olive drab, which was standard on Ninth Air Force Havocs. This aircraft also includes the black-and-white 'invasion stripes', applied as an Allied identification feature.

Douglas A-20B

An A-20B (41-3134) from 84th Bomb Squadron,
47th Bomb Group, based at Mediouna, Morocco,
December 1942.

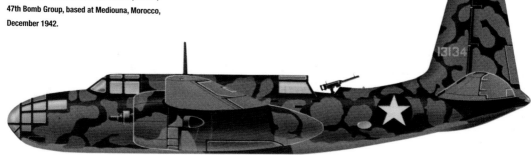

parachute failed to open after he had
bailed out. French observer Maurice
Chemidlin was trapped in the fuselage
but survived, though with serious
injuries. Despite the loss of the aircraft,
the French were impressed enough to
order 100 production examples on 15
February, following this up after the
outbreak of war with an order for 170
more in October.

Many changes were stipulated by
the French: the fuselage was deepened
and narrowed to allow for greater fuel
capacity and the interchangeable nose
was discarded, with French aircraft
standardizing a glazed bombardier
nose of better streamlined form than
the prototype with four fixed 7.5mm
(0.29in) machine guns. Additionally, the
wing lost its slight rearward sweep and
was mounted higher on the fuselage.

As a result, the engines were slung
lower under the wing to keep the main
undercarriage legs short. In this form,
the aircraft became the DB-7, and the
first example flew on 17 August 1939,
with production aircraft arriving in
France from October.

Around 70 of the 270 DB-7s on
order for the Armée de l'Air were
delivered before the French armistice,
and of those, only a few saw combat,
entering the war for the first time in May
1940. All surviving DB-7s were flown to

North Africa just before the armistice
and formed four squadrons of the Vichy
French Air Force, bombing Gibraltar in
July 1940 in retaliation for the British
attack on French vessels at Mers-el-
Kébir. After French forces in North
Africa joined the Allies, these aircraft
were used for a variety of training and
ancillary roles, though a few of these
by now quite old aircraft carried out
attacks against German strongholds
along the Atlantic coast of France
between October 1944 and April 1945.

**Britain, Belgium and
the Netherlands**

When France capitulated in June 1940,
the DB-7 order was taken over by the
British Purchasing Commission along
with an order for 16 aircraft for Belgium
and undelivered aircraft were taken
on strength by the RAF, which named
them 'Boston' if used as a bomber
and 'Havoc' (after briefly being known
as 'Ranger') if adapted for the night
fighter role. Earlier-production DB-7s
with 746kW (1000hp) R-1830-SC3-
Gs, designated Boston Mk I, were
judged unfit for combat by the British
and used only for training and other
second-line roles. Later-production
DB-7s that featured more powerful
820kW (1100hp) R-1830-S3C4-G
engines were designated Mk II, and

Douglas A-20B

Weight (Maximum take-off): 10,795kg (23,800lb)

Dimensions: Length 14.63m (48ft), Wingspan 18.69m
(61ft 4in), Height 5.51m (18ft 1in)

Powerplant: Two 1194kW (1600hp) Wright R-2600-
11 Twin Cyclone 14-cylinder air-cooled radial piston
engines

Maximum speed: 563km/h (350mph)

Range: 1328km (825 miles)

Ceiling: 8717m (28,600ft)

Crew: 3

Armament: Two 12.7mm (0.5in) Browning M2
machine guns fixed forward-firing on each side of
forward fuselage, one 12.7mm flexible machine
gun in the top gunner's position, one 7.62mm (0.3in)
Browning M1919 machine gun flexibly mounted in
ventral tunnel position; 1089kg (2400lb) bomb load

these were the first to see operational
use in British hands. The short range
of the ex-French aircraft precluded its
use against German targets from British
bases, so most of these aircraft were
utilized as Havoc Mk I night fighters
and intruders equipped with airborne
radar. Further development for an
improved version for France saw the
aircraft re-engined with the 1193kW
(1600hp) Wright R-2600-A5B Double
Cyclone and fitted with larger vertical
tail surfaces as the DB-7A, resulting in
enhanced performance, and this variant
entered production for the RAF as
the Boston Mk III, though most would

be converted to night fighters as the Havoc Mk II.

Confusingly, the same Boston III designation was then used for DB-7Bs, DB-73s (a similar model ordered by France) and ex-USAAF A-20Cs in British service. The DB-7B was the first Boston variant built to a British rather than a French contract, and 300 were on order by April 1940. A further 48 were ordered by the Netherlands government in exile for use in the Netherlands East Indies, but only one aircraft of the first six delivered was ready in time to take part in action against the Japanese advance, with the rest being captured.

Twenty-two DB-7Bs of the remaining 26 on NEI order were taken on instead by the RAAF and saw much action in the New Guinea theatre, subsequently receiving A-20As, Cs and Gs as combat attrition replacements.

US specifications

As the DB-7 was being introduced to active service with the French and British, the first production aircraft tailored to a US order were being built. The improvements to the aircraft driven by French requirements were sufficient to overcome American indifference, and the Douglas was ordered as the A-20, with turbo-supercharged engines for high-altitude operations, and the A-20A, essentially identical to the British DB-7B except for being fitted with American gun armament and radio, intended for medium and low level with two-stage mechanical superchargers. Problems with the turbo superchargers meant that only one

A-20 was built, and except for three built as F-3 reconnaissance aircraft, the remaining 59 A-20s on order were completed as P-70 night fighters. Meanwhile, the first A-20A was delivered in November 1940, entering service in the spring of 1941 with the 3rd Light Bombardment Group at Savannah, Georgia. An unusual feature of the A-20/A-20A aircraft was the provision for a fixed rearward-firing 7.62mm (0.3in) machine gun in each engine nacelle. These guns were fired by the rear gunner using a pedal, though were rarely actually fitted.

The first variant to be ordered in large numbers by the USAAC (a total of 999) was the A-20B, which, although slightly faster, was in most regards a backwards step when compared to the A-20A. Based on the earlier DB-7A airframe, the A-20B lacked self-sealing fuel tanks and carried less armour protection. Following experience in the Pacific with other, better-protected A-20 variants, most of the A-20Bs were supplied through lend-lease channels to the USSR, the first of many A-20s to be used by the Soviets. The A-20B was followed by a variant intended to be a standardized aircraft for use by both the US and UK: the A-20C.

As it turned out, very few A-20Cs entered US service, and those that did were virtually all used for training. However, the RAF utilized the aircraft extensively as the Boston III (later production blocks were designated Boston IIIA), and an even greater number were supplied to the Soviet Union. In Soviet service, the A-20C's ability to carry a torpedo was regularly employed in anti-shipping operations.

A-20G

The A-20D was a proposed high-speed variant that was never built. The A-20E was a designation used to cover 17 A-20As utilized on various trials work. A single XA-20F was built with a remotely controlled defensive turret system that did not enter production but was used on the A-26 Invader that would succeed the A-20 in US units. The A-20G, however, was built in larger numbers than any other A-20 subtype, with 2850 built in 1943 and 1944.

First delivered during February 1943, the A-20G introduced a solid nose armed with four 20mm (0.79in) M2 cannon and two 12.7mm (0.5in) machine guns. This new nose was introduced because of combat experience in the Pacific, where glass-nosed A-20s had been fitted in field modifications

This A-20G-20 served with a unit of the Ninth Air Force, which took its place alongside the Eighth Air Force in operations in the ETO, and flew more than 100,000 combat missions in the run-up to D-Day.

developed by Major Paul 'Pappy' Gunn to increase their forward firepower during low-level strafing missions, achieving conspicuous success, notably in the Battle of the Bismarck Sea. The 20mm (0.79in) weapons proved unpopular due to their slow rate of fire and propensity to jam, so – after 250 aircraft were constructed – the cannon were replaced with four 12.7mm (0.5in) machine guns and nearly all of the cannon-armed A-20Gs were supplied to the Soviet Union.

Later-production A-20Gs saw their defensive capability improved with the addition of a Martin-designed dorsal turret in place of the handheld rear gun seen with earlier A-20s. The turret required the fuselage in the vicinity of the rear cockpit to be widened by 15cm (6in), and this, combined with an increased bomb and fuel load, improved armour protection and a switch from a 7.62mm (0.3in) to a 12.7mm (0.5in) gun in the ventral position, saw a considerable increase in the weight of the aircraft, resulting in a reduction in top speed.

The majority of A-20Gs were supplied to the USSR, some of which were fitted with Soviet-designed turrets and used in low-level attacks against German targets, suffering heavy losses to flak. USAAF A-20Gs were used in a similar fashion by the Ninth Air Force supporting operations in France and also suffered heavy losses, subsequently switching to less dangerous medium-level operations. However, Japanese flak defences were not as effective as their German equivalents, and during low-level attack sorties in New Guinea, A-20s were used to great effect against Japanese targets on land and sea, utilizing strafing and skip-bombing attacks against enemy shipping.

A-20H

The A-20G was followed by the A-20H, identical except for the addition of 1270kw (1700hp) R-2600-29 engines, and 412 A-20Hs were built, after which production switched to the A-20J, which re-introduced a Perspex bombardier nose, though now of an improved frameless design, and was fitted with a Norden bombsight. The A-20J was intended to operate as a 'lead ship' for formations of solid-nose A-20G or A-20Hs, all aircraft dropping their bombs on a signal from the bombardier in the leading aircraft. Of the 450 built, 169 were supplied to the RAF as the Boston IV.

The final production version of the A-20 series was the A-20K, identical to the A-20J but featuring the same R-2600-29 engines as the A-20H.

Four hundred and thirteen A-20ks were built, and 90 were supplied to the RAF as the Boston V. RAF Bostons saw much action in Western Europe until after D-Day when units gradually transitioned to more capable bombers. Only the Free French-manned 342 squadron retained the Boston until VE Day.

In the Mediterranean, however, RAF Bostons were retained beyond the end of the war, and a Boston V carried out the final night raid in Italy on 30 April 1945. Even as the superior A-26 Invader was being introduced to operations in Europe, the A-20J (and K) was retained as a lead ship in A-26 units pending the development of the Invader's A-26C variant with a bombardier nose position. Forty-six A-20J and Ks were also converted to F-3A unarmed night reconnaissance aircraft, which saw operational use in the last year of the war.

The largest user of the A-20 was the USSR, which received over two-thirds of total A-20 production, and it became the most numerous foreign bomber operated by the Soviets, with 900 still in Soviet service at VJ-Day. Subsequently, the A-20 received the NATO reporting name 'Box'. The final user of all was Brazil, which received 31 lend-lease A-20s in 1944, retiring the last of them in 1955.

Douglas A-26 Invader

Representing a considerable technological leap in this class of aircraft, the A-26 entered service only very late in the war but proved highly effective. It subsequently remained in frontline USAF service until 1972.

Designed by a team led by the brilliant Ed Heinemann, the A-26 took shape as a larger and more powerful replacement for the highly successful A-20. First flown on 10 July 1942 by veteran racing pilot Benny Howard (himself a successful aircraft designer), flight testing revealed that the XA-26 possessed excellent performance and handling. Relatively minor issues with engine cooling were dealt with by altering the cowlings and dispensing with propeller spinners, and the nosewheel was redesigned after being found to possess inadequate strength.

Overall, however, testing proved remarkably trouble-free, though the sighting and control system of the dorsal and ventral remotely controlled turrets, both controlled by the same crewman proved difficult to develop and work effectively. This novel and advanced defensive system would also prove difficult to maintain in the field.

The first production aircraft was delivered to the USAAF in September 1943, and a batch of early A-26s was sent to the South West Pacific Area for evaluation under combat conditions. These aircraft were all examples of the initial A-26B variant, the first to enter production with a 'solid' nose featuring a heavy forward-firing gun armament (the A-26A being a night fighter development that remained a prototype). The first mission was flown on 23 June 1944, when four aircraft bombed Japanese positions in the Netherlands East Indies.

However, the aircraft proved unpopular in the Pacific due to the position of the engines, which hindered the downward view, rendering the A-26B unsuitable for its intended role of ground attack and leading General George Kenney, commander of Far East Air Forces, to state: "We do not want the A-26 under any circumstances as a replacement

for anything", which was hardly an auspicious assessment for the new Douglas bomber. However, trials in Europe would prove radically different.

The first 18 evaluation aircraft arrived in the summer of 1944, flying their first mission on 6 September. During eight test missions, no aircraft were lost, and the Ninth Air Force undertook to replace both the A-20 and B-26 with the new aircraft.

The first group to convert was the 416th Bombardment Group, which entered combat with their A-26Bs on 17 November 1944. A shortage of A-26C variants with a bombardier nose saw Invader units utilize A-20s as lead ships until the glass-nosed version began to be delivered in quantity.

In bombing, strafing, tactical reconnaissance and night interdiction missions, A-26s proved highly effective. In marked contrast to the experience in the Pacific, the A-26 was well received by pilots and crew alike, and by VE Day, A-26s had dropped 18,054 US tons (16,120 tonnes) of bombs and achieved seven confirmed air-to-air kills, while losing 67 aircraft. From January 1945, some units of the Twelfth Air Force in Italy also received A-26s, flying direct support and interdiction against tanks and troop concentrations in the last few months of the war.

Postwar, the A-26 was redesignated B-26 in 1948, following the dropping of the 'A' for 'attack' prefix. The B-26 saw much active service during the Korean War and subsequently in Vietnam, upgraded to B-26K standard, where it was used as a highly effective counter-insurgency aircraft. B-26s were also used by many postwar air forces as well as the CIA, before being widely employed as a firefighting aircraft.

Douglas A-26B Invader

Weight (Maximum take-off): 15,876kg (35,000lb)

Dimensions: Length: 15.24m (50ft), Wingspan: 21.34m (70ft), Height: 5.64m (18ft 6in)

Powerplant: Two 1491kW (2000hp) Pratt & Whitney R-2800-71 or R-2800-27 or R-2800-79 Double Wasp 18-cylinder air-cooled radial piston engines

Range: 4184km (2600 miles)

Ceiling: 8687m (28,500ft)

Crew: 3

Armament: Six eight 12.7mm (0.5in) Browning M2 machine guns fixed forward-firing in nose, two 12.7mm (0.5in) Browning M2 machine guns in both remote controlled dorsal and ventral turrets, up to eight 12.7mm (0.5in) Browning M2 machine guns fixed forward-firing in four underwing pods or three 12.7mm (0.5in) Browning M2 machine guns fixed forward-firing in each wing; up to 1800kg (4000lb) in bomb bay plus up to 910kg (2000lb) on underwing hardpoints

---

Douglas A-26B Invader

This A-26B was part of 552nd Bombardment Squadron, 386th Bomb Group, US Ninth Army Air Force, based at Beaumont-sur-Oise, France, April 1945.

Douglas A-26 Invader

CUTAWAY KEY

1 Starboard wing tip
2 Starboard navigation light
3 Water tank
4 Water tank filler cap
5 Aileron hinge control
6 Starboard aileron
7 Aileron tab
8 Landing and taxiing light
9 Control cables
10 Bombardier nose configuration, A-26C
11 Optically flat bomb sight window
12 Bomb bay doors
13 Ventral periscope gunsight
14 Ventral turret
15 Starboard outboard flap
16 Wing access panels
17 Chordwise stiffeners
18 Double slotted flap segments
19 Oil cooler radiator
20 Cooler intake ducting
21 Ram air intake to oil cooler
22 Nacelle fuel tank, capacity 1136 litres (300 US gal)
23 Wing inboard fuel tank, capacity 379 litres (100 US gal)
24 Control runs
25 Oil tank filler
26 Oil tank
27 Carburettor intake ducting
28 Exhaust stubs
29 Cowling air flaps
30 Pratt & Whitney R-2800-27 Double Wasp, two-row 18-cylinder radial engine
31 Carburettor ram air intake
32 Propeller reduction gearbox
33 Propeller hub mechanism
34 Three-bladed propeller
35 Detachable engine cowlings
36 General purpose nose configuration, A-26B
37 Machine-gun barrels
38 Four 12.7mm (0.5in) machine-guns, starboard side
39 Spent cartridge case chutes
40 Gun bay bracing strut
41 Two 12.7mm (0.5in) machine-guns, port side
42 Ammunition feed chutes
43 Ammunition boxes
44 Pitot tube
45 Nosewheel torque scissors
46 Rearward retracting nosewheel
47 Shock absorber leg strut
48 Nosewheel doors
49 Nosewheel bay/flight deck floor support construction
50 Rudder pedals
51 Interchangeable nose joint bulkhead
52 Autopilot controls
53 Back of instrument panel
54 Fixed foresight
55 Windscreen panels
56 Instrument panel shroud
57 Reflector sight
58 Clear vision panel
59 Control column
60 Pilot's seat
61 Pilot's side window panel/entry hatch
62 Bomb release controls
63 Bombardier/navigator's seat
64 Canopy hatch handles
65 Bombardier/navigator's side canopy/ entry hatch
66 Oxygen regulator
67 Radio racks
68 Radio receivers and transmitters
69 Bomb-bay armoured roof panel
70 Wing root fillet
71 Armoured wing spar bulkhead
72 Hydraulic accumulators
73 Air filter
74 De-icing valve
75 Aerial mast
76 Double slotted flap inboard section
77 Wing de-icing fluid reservoir
78 De-icing fluid pump
79 Starboard bomb rack, five 45kg (100lb) HE bombs
80 Port bomb rack, five 45kg (100lb) HE bombs
81 Bomb launcher rails
82 Rear wing spar bulkhead
83 Turret drive motor
84 Upper remotely controlled gun turret
85 Two 12.7mm (0.5in) machine-guns
86 Turret mechanism
87 Ammunition boxes
88 Port aft bomb rack, three 45kg (100lb) HE bombs
89 Inboard double slotted flap
90 Gunner's bomb bay entry hatch
91 Oxygen cylinders
92 Life raft
93 Gunner's canopy cover
94 Ditching hatch
95 Upper periscope sight
96 Periscope eyepiece
97 Turret controls
98 Oxygen bottles
99 Gunner's armoured bulkhead
100 Ventral turret ammunition
101 Cabin heater
102 D/F loop antenna fairing
103 Fin root fillet
104 Tailplane control cables
105 Cable pulleys
106 Fin rib construction
107 Starboard tailplane
108 Starboard elevator
109 Fin leading edge
110 Aerial cables
111 Fin tip fairing
112 Fabric covered rudder construction
113 Rudder tab
114 Trim tab control
115 Rudder hinge post
116 Tail navigation lights
117 Elevator tab
118 Port elevator
119 Port tailplane construction
120 Elevator control horns
121 Tailplane root fillet
122 Fin/tailplane fixing frame
123 Rear fuselage construction
124 Oxygen bottles
125 Rear fuselage construction joint bulkhead
126 Turret control amplifier
127 Turret covers
128 Ventral turret control mechanism
129 Two 12.7mm (0.5in) machine-guns
130 Port nacelle tailcone
131 Aft nacelle construction
132 Engine fire extinguishers
133 Main undercarriage wheel well
134 Outboard double slotted flaps
135 Flap hinge links
136 Wing rear spar
137 Aileron tab
138 Port aileron
139 Fabric covered aileron construction
140 Port wing tip
141 Port navigation light
142 Wing rib construction
143 Leading edge stiffeners
144 Aileron hinge control
145 Landing and taxiing lamp housing
146 Wing leading edge
147 Fluid de-iced leading edge
148 Mainwheel doors
149 Main undercarriage door link mechanism
150 Retraction jack
151 Main undercarriage leg
152 Rearward retracting mainwheel
153 Access panel
154 Nacelle fuel tank, capacity 1136 litres (300 US gal)
155 Oil cooler ram air intake
156 Oil tank filler cap
157 Engine compartment bulkhead/ firewall
158 Engine mounting struts
159 Exhaust ducts
160 Cowling cooling air flaps
161 Engine mounting bulkhead
162 Carburettor intake ducting
163 Cowling construction
164 Propeller hub mechanism
165 Three bladed propeller

SPECIFICATION A-26 INVADER

Crew

Three

Powerplant

two Pratt & Whitney R-2800-27 or -79 radial piston engines each rated at 1491kW (2000hp)

Performance:

maximum speed 571km/h (355mph) at 4570m (15,000ft); cruising speed 457km/h (284mph) at optimum altitude; climb to 3050m (10,000ft) in 8 minutes 6 seconds; service ceiling 6735m (22,100ft); range 2253km (1,400 miles) with standard fuel and warload

Weights

empty 10,147kg (22,370lb); maximum take-off 15,876kg (35,000lb)

Dimensions

Wingspan 21.34m (70ft); length 15.24m (50ft); height 5.64m (18ft 6in); wing area 50.17m² (540.00 sq ft)

Armament

Six 12.7mm (0.5in) Browning M2 fixed forward-firing machine-guns in the forward fuselage, two 12.7mm (0.5in) Browning M2 trainable machine-guns in the dorsal barbette that could be locked to fire directly forward under pilot control, two 12.7mm (0.5in) Browning M2 trainable rearward-firing machine-guns in the optional ventral barbette, and provision for eight 12.7mm (0.5in) Browning M2 fixed forward-firing machine-guns installed in four two-gun packs under the outboard wing panels; plus up to 2722kg (6,000lb) of disposable stores carried in two lower-fuselage weapons bays and on four underwing hardpoints

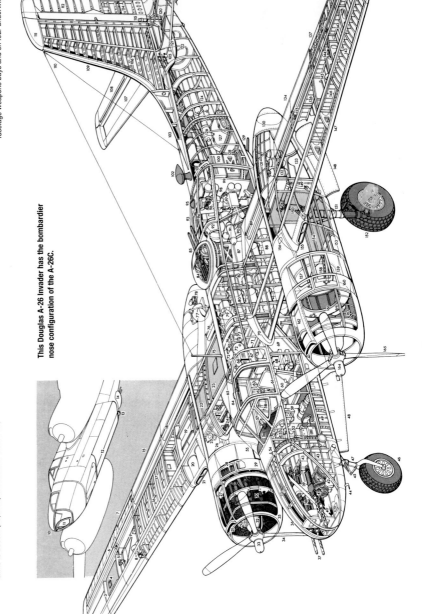

This Douglas A-26 Invader has the bombardier nose configuration of the A-26C.

North American B-25 Mitchell

The outstanding American medium bomber of World War II, the B-25 was dependable, easy to fly and possessed an almost unbelievable ability to absorb battle damage and keep flying.

The B-25 was North American Aviation's response to the US Army Air Corps-issued Proposal Circular 38-385 for an 'Aircraft – Bombardment Type – Medium', which was intended to provide a superior bomber to the B-18 Bolo and called for an aircraft capable of carrying a payload of 1100kg (2400lb) for 1900km (1200 miles) at 480km/h (300mph). North American had already developed the NA-40 as their entry into an earlier light bomber competition that had been won by the Douglas A-20 and developed this basic design in response to the new requirement.

NA-62 and Dutch roll

Under the supervision of chief engineer Lee Atwood, the NA-40 design was somewhat enlarged in all dimensions while retaining the same layout as the original aircraft, resulting in the NA-62. The tandem cockpit was discarded in favour of a side-by-side seating arrangement for pilot and co-pilot necessitating the use of a wider fuselage, and the wing was lowered from the high shoulder position on the NA-40B to a mid-fuselage position, retaining the continuous three-degree dihedral of the original design. Impressed with the design, the Air Corps ordered 184 NA-62s 'off the drawing board' in September 1939 as the B-25, and after approval of a full-size B-25 mock-up in November, the first B-25 (there being no XB-25 prototype as such) was complete by the summer of 1940.

The aircraft was flown for the first time by test pilot Vance Breese on 19 August 1940, and while generally satisfactory, USAAC tests revealed that the aircraft was susceptible to 'Dutch roll': a motion in which the aircraft rolls in one direction and yaws in the other. This was cured by reducing the dihedral of the wing panels outboard of the engine nacelles to an extremely slight angle of anhedral, giving the B-25 its characteristic gull-wing appearance.

Only the first nine aircraft were built with constant dihedral wings. Less obvious changes were made to the tail fins, which went through a series of slightly different designs before settling on the broadly rectangular units with a slightly swept leading edge that would remain standard throughout the aircraft's production life.

'Billy' Mitchell

The idea to name the aircraft after the great proponent of air power General William 'Billy' Mitchell, who had died in 1936, apparently came from Lee Atwood himself, and the Air Corps readily agreed. The first B-25 was accepted by the Army in February of 1941, and the first unit to receive the Mitchell was the 17th Bombardment

The definitive B-25J was built in both solid- and glass-nosed versions. Both types often served in the same unit; these aircraft are from 47th Bomb Squadron, 41st Bomb Group, seen on Okinawa in July 1945. Both carry Mk 13 glide torpedoes.

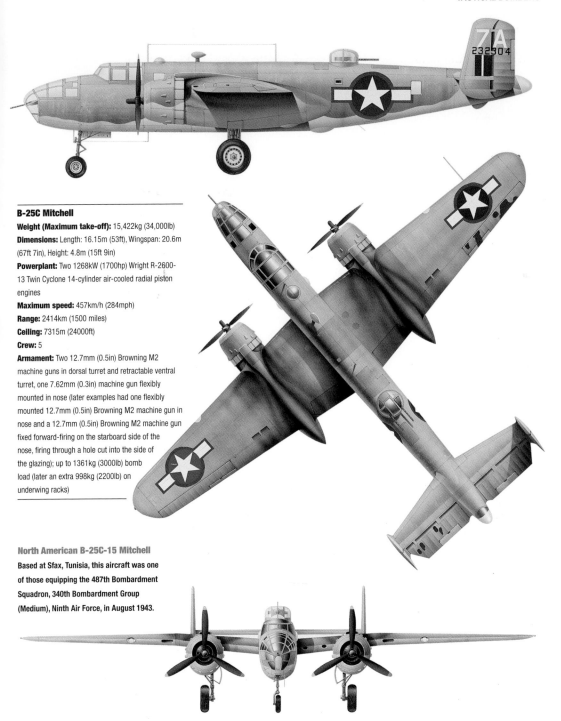

B-25C Mitchell

Weight (Maximum take-off): 15,422kg (34,000lb)

Dimensions: Length: 16.15m (53ft), Wingspan: 20.6m (67ft 7in), Height: 4.8m (15ft 9in)

Powerplant: Two 1268kW (1700hp) Wright R-2600-13 Twin Cyclone 14-cylinder air-cooled radial piston engines

Maximum speed: 457km/h (284mph)

Range: 2414km (1500 miles)

Ceiling: 7315m (24000ft)

Crew: 5

Armament: Two 12.7mm (0.5in) Browning M2 machine guns in dorsal turret and retractable ventral turret, one 7.62mm (0.3in) machine gun flexibly mounted in nose (later examples had one flexibly mounted 12.7mm (0.5in) Browning M2 machine gun in nose and a 12.7mm (0.5in) Browning M2 machine gun fixed forward-firing on the starboard side of the nose, firing through a hole cut into the side of the glazing); up to 1361kg (3000lb) bomb load (later an extra 998kg (2200lb) on underwing racks)

North American B-25C-15 Mitchell
Based at Sfax, Tunisia, this aircraft was one of those equipping the 487th Bombardment Squadron, 340th Bombardment Group (Medium), Ninth Air Force, in August 1943.

North American B-25G Mitchell

This B-25G (serial no. 264758) is shown from the Army Air Forces Tactical Centre, Orlando Field, Florida.

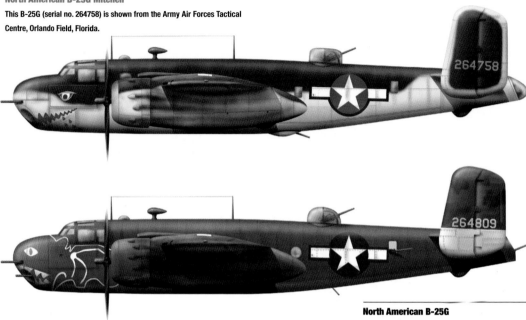

North American B-25G Mitchell

This B-25G from the 499th Bombardment Squadron, 345th Bomb Group, operated from Biak Island in the Netherlands East Indies. In July 1944 the 499th moved to Biak Island, where it attacked Japanese airfields and shipping in the Philippines.

North American B-25G

Weight (Maximum take-off): 15,876kg (35,000lb)

Dimensions: Length: 15.49m (50ft 10in), Wingspan: 20.6m (67ft 7in), Height: 4.98m (16ft 4in)

Powerplant: Two 1268 kw (1700hp) Wright R-2600-13 Twin Cyclone fourteen-cylinder air-cooled radial piston engines

Maximum speed: 451km/h (280mph)

Range: 2511km (1560 miles)

Ceiling: 7410m (24,310ft)

Crew: 5

Armament: One 75mm M4 cannon fixed forward-firing in nose, two 12.7mm (0.5in) machine guns fixed forward-firing in nose, two 12.7mm (0.5in) Browning M2 machine guns in dorsal turret, and retractable ventral turret; up to 1361kg (3000lb) bomb load

North American B-25G Mitchell

This B-25G Mitchell (serial no. 264842), flew with the 279th Bombardment Squadron, 310th Bomb Group, based in Oran, Algeria, August–September 1943.

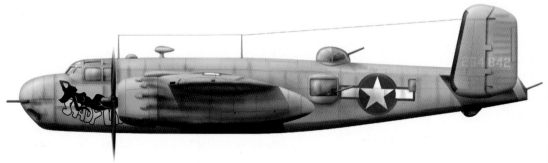

North American B-25G Mitchell

B-25G (serial no. 264895) was part of the 48th Bombardment Squadron, 41st
Bomb Group. The 41st Bombardment Group was activated 15 January 1941 at
March Field, California. This aircraft is shown from 1944, when the group was
involved in neutralizing Japanese forces in the Marshall Islands.

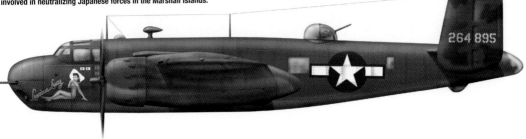

North American B-25G Mitchell

This aircraft (serial no. 265217) served with the 823rd Bombardment Squadron
'Tigers', 28th Bomb Group, based at Nadzab, New Guinea, circa 1944.

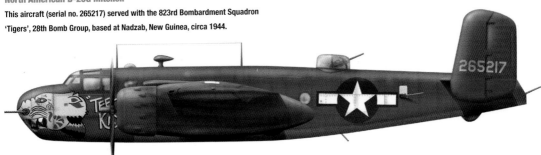

Group at McChord Field in Washington state. North American built 24 of the initial B-25 model before switching to the B-25A, which introduced self-sealing fuel tanks and increased crew armour – features that the fighting in Europe had revealed to be essential in any modern combat aircraft. Forty B-25As were built before the B-25B began rolling off the production line.

The B-25B saw the cramped prone tail gunner position and its single 12.7mm (0.5in) gun removed and a dorsal and remotely operated ventral turret added instead, each fitted with two 12.7mm (0.5in) weapons, with the prone position at the end of the tail retained for observation. The ventral turret, however, proved difficult to use in combat and was often removed.

The Doolittle Raid

Few B-25Bs saw combat in US hands, but 16 aircraft were used to perform the Mitchell's first, and most famous, mission: the Doolittle Raid. Following the attack on Pearl Harbor, there was a great drive to retaliate against the Japanese mainland. No land-based bombers were based sufficiently close to Japan to be able to undertake such a mission, and the short range of the Navy's carrier aircraft would require their carriers to sail dangerously close to the Japanese coast. The idea of launching USAAF bombers from a carrier on a one-way mission was devised by Captain Francis S. Low of the US Navy, and the B-25 was selected over the B-18 or B-23 because its wingspan was short

enough to allow clearance for carrier take-off. The B-25 was also chosen over the B-26 due to its superior take-off characteristics.

On 2 February 1942, the first trial take-off was made by a B-25 from the carrier Hornet. After sailing from San Francisco, the carrier was spotted on 18 April and forced to launch the strike aircraft early. The B-25s, led by noted pre-war racing pilot Colonel James Doolittle, attacked a variety of targets in Japan, including Tokyo and the Yokosuka Naval dockyard, before flying on to crash-land in China (though one aircraft made it to the Soviet Union, where it was interned and operated by the USSR). The damage inflicted by the raid was insignificant. However, as a propaganda exercise, the raid was a

North American B-25H Mitchell

B-25H (serial no. 34380) flew as part of the USAAF's 1st Air Commando Group (1st ACG), from Hailakandi, India. Formed in March 1944, the group was organized to provide fighter cover, bombardment striking power, and air transportation services for Wingate's Chindits fighting in Burma.

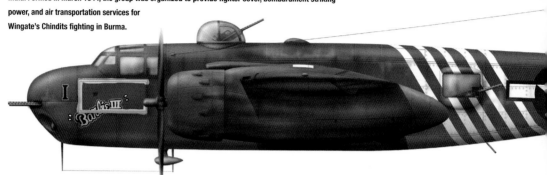

huge success, especially in boosting civilian morale in the US.

B-25C and D

Despite being built in trivial numbers, the B-25B was the first B-25 model to be exported. Of the 120 built, 23 examples were supplied to the RAF, which adopted the USAAF name for the aircraft, designating the B-25B the Mitchell Mk I. The RAF used all of these aircraft for training and would ultimately receive over 900 Mitchells of various subtypes, making it the second largest operator of the type.

The B-25C that followed the B-25B into production was the first of the truly mass-produced variants, with 1619 rolling off the assembly line between December 1941 and May 1943. The main difference between the new model and the outwardly identical B-25B was its adoption of a later engine subtype, the R-2600-13 Double Cyclone, along with a new 24-volt electrical system. Armament initially remained the same as the earlier aircraft, but later the flexible 7.62mm (0.3in) Browning gun in the nose would be replaced by a 12.7mm (0.5in) weapon and augmented by a second, fixed, forward-firing 12.7mm

(0.5in) gun mounted on the starboard side of the nose and firing through a hole cut into the Plexiglas glazing. At the same time as the B-25C was being built, North American's new factory in Kansas started production of a near-identical variant designated the B-25D to distinguish it from the Inglewood, California-produced B-25C. The B-25D was also built in great numbers: 2290 were eventually built. The B-25C was the first Mitchell variant to see significant combat, mostly against Japanese targets with USAAF units, though the aircraft was used throughout the Mediterranean. Only the RAF would use the Mitchell from British bases against targets in Western Europe, US tactical bombing units having standardized on the B-26 Marauder for this type of mission. In total, 167 B-25Bs and 371 B-25Ds were supplied to the RAF, where they were known as the Mitchell II.

B-25E and F

The B-25E and F designations were used by B-25C aircraft fitted with experimental de-icing systems. Only one of each was converted, but the B-25G saw a major change to the basic design, and unusually, it was

North American B-25H

Weight (Maximum take-off): 15,876kg (35,000lb)

Dimensions: Length: 15.49m (50ft 10in), Wingspan: 20.6m (67ft 7in), Height: 4.98m (16ft 4in)

Powerplant: Two 1268 kw (1700hp) Wright R-2600-13 Twin Cyclone 14-cylinder air-cooled radial piston engines

Maximum speed: 441km/h (275mph)

Range: 2173km (1350 miles)

Ceiling: 7560m (24,800ft)

Crew: 5

Armament: One 75mm T13E1 cannon fixed forward-firing in nose, four 12.7mm (0.5in) Browning M2 machine guns fixed forward-firing in nose, four 12.7mm (0.5in) machine guns fixed forward-firing in blisters on starboard and port sides of aircraft, two 12.7mm (0.5in) Browning M2 machine guns in dorsal turret, two 12.7mm (0.5in) machine guns flexibly mounted in waist position, two 12.7mm (0.5in) machine guns flexibly mounted in tail turret; up to 1450kg (3200lb) bomb load

predated by a field modification. The requirements of anti-shipping combat operations in the Pacific had seen Major Paul 'Pappy' Gunn successfully add more guns to the Douglas A-20, but the limited capacity of this comparatively small aircraft limited the amount of extra firepower that could be added. Gunn and a North American field service representative, Jack Fox, felt that the

Rabaul, all the transports and four of the destroyers were sunk or beached. The B-25 strafers achieved a 43 per cent hit ratio.

B-25G gunship variant

North American developed its own 'gunship' variant: the B-25G. Like the extemporized strafing Mitchells developed by Gunn, the B-25G dispensed with the bombardier position and featured a new, shorter nose armed with two 12.7mm (0.5in) Browning guns and a colossal M4 75mm (3in) cannon, derived from the famed French 75 field gun of World War I. This weapon was the largest calibre gun to be used by an operational aircraft during World War II and had been trialled on a modified B-18 Bolo. First fitted to a converted B-25C, a further five C models were so modified, followed by 400 new-build B-25Gs, which also featured increased armour and a greater fuel supply. Combat results with the B-25G proved a mixed bag.

Although the 75mm (3in) gun was a highly powerful and accurate weapon capable of inflicting meaningful damage (even to a destroyer), the hand-loaded weapon's slow rate of fire – in action, it proved generally impossible to fire more than four shots per attack – required a long, straight

run into the target, leaving the aircraft vulnerable to return fire. Furthermore, the two machine guns, added primarily to assist in aiming the 75mm (3in) weapon, proved inadequate in providing suppressing fire.

B-25H

These concerns were addressed by the B-25H, of which 1000 were built, and which utilized an updated 75mm (3in) weapon, the T13E-1 (derived from the gun fitted to the Sherman tank) and included four 12.7mm (0.5in) machine guns in the nose. This variant re-introduced tail armament in the form of an armour-protected twin-gun rear gun position, necessitating a deepened rear fuselage to allow a seat for the gunner to be fitted (rather than the earlier prone position). The dorsal turret was moved forward to a position just aft of the flight deck, a flexibly mounted 12.7mm (0.5in) gun was provided on each side of the rear fuselage (both operated by one gunner) and the troublesome ventral turret, which had often been discarded in service, was finally deleted. By the time the B-25H entered operational service, the hardened or armoured targets the 75mm (3in) weapon was intended for were largely absent from the Pacific theatre, and many examples of this and the B-25G saw the larger weapon replaced with a further pair of

B-25 could make a much more potent gunship, and General George Kenney, commander of Allied Air Forces in the South West Pacific Area, gave the project his blessing.

Following successful trials, 12 B-25s were modified with eight fixed forward-firing 12.7mm (0.5in) guns in the nose and mounted on the fuselage sides. These aircraft proved particularly successful – in concert with US B-17s and A-20s, and RAAF Beauforts and Beaufighters – in the Battle of the Bismarck Sea in March 1943, utilizing their intense firepower to prevent return fire from the ships they were subjecting to skip bombing attack. Out of the original convoy of eight destroyers and eight cargo vessels that had departed

North American B-25H Mitchell
This aircraft (serial no. 34935), was part of the 1st Air Commando Group (1st ACG), flying from Chittagong Airfield, January 1945.

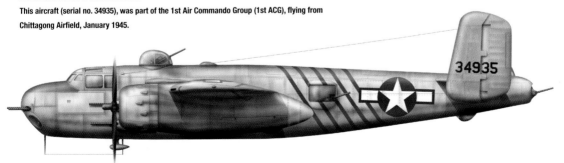

North American B-25D Mitchell

This B-25D of the 340th Bombardment Group
operated from bases in Algeria during the North
African, Sicily and Italian campaigns of 1942–43.
'Dirty Gerty From Bizerte' (serial no. 41-29896) was
named for a popular soldier's ditty of the period. It
is painted in RAF Desert Pink over medium grey.

Gull wing
The Mitchell bomber had a
characteristic inverted gull wing,
which made the aircraft much more
manoeuvrable.

Nose section
The glazed nose section housed the
bombardier, who was equipped with a
Norden bombsight. His escape hatch was
at the rear of the compartment, on the
port side. The bombardier also operated
two machine guns, one fixed forward-
firing, and the other on a flexible mount.

Bomb load
The Mitchell bomber could carry
1361kg (3000lb) of bombs in its two
vertical bomb bays.

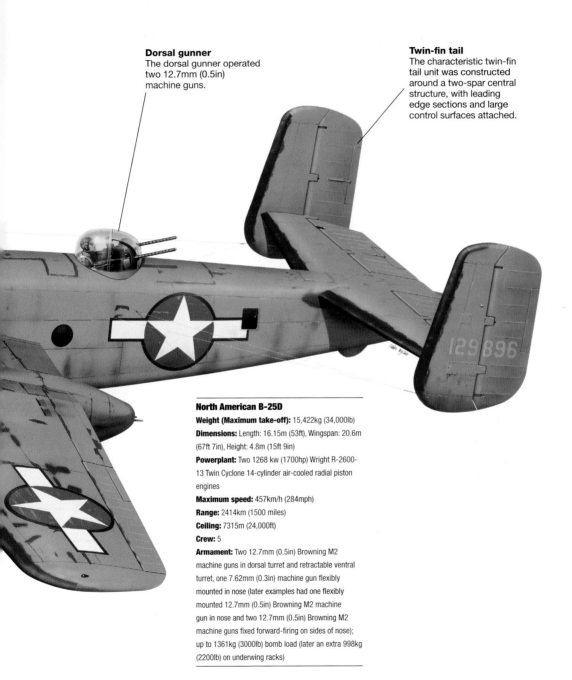

Dorsal gunner
The dorsal gunner operated
two 12.7mm (0.5in)
machine guns.

Twin-fin tail
The characteristic twin-fin
tail unit was constructed
around a two-spar central
structure, with leading
edge sections and large
control surfaces attached.

North American B-25D
Weight (Maximum take-off): 15,422kg (34,000lb)
Dimensions: Length: 16.15m (53ft), Wingspan: 20.6m
(67ft 7in), Height: 4.8m (15ft 9in)
Powerplant: Two 1268 kw (1700hp) Wright R-2600-
13 Twin Cyclone 14-cylinder air-cooled radial piston
engines
Maximum speed: 457km/h (284mph)
Range: 2414km (1500 miles)
Ceiling: 7315m (24,000ft)
Crew: 5
Armament: Two 12.7mm (0.5in) Browning M2
machine guns in dorsal turret and retractable ventral
turret, one 7.62mm (0.3in) machine gun flexibly
mounted in nose (later examples had one flexibly
mounted 12.7mm (0.5in) Browning M2 machine
gun in nose and two 12.7mm (0.5in) Browning M2
machine guns fixed forward-firing on sides of nose);
up to 1361kg (3000lb) bomb load (later an extra 998kg
(2200lb) on underwing racks)

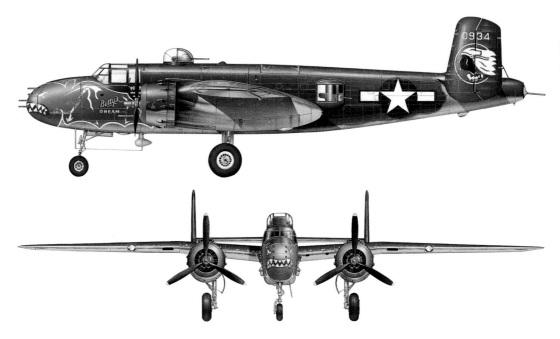

North American B-25J Mitchell
This aircraft flew in the southwest Pacific with the USAAF's 499th Bomb Squadron, otherwise known as the 'Bats Outa Hell'. The front end of the aircraft was painted with a huge bat figure with teeth and wings.

North American B-25J
Weight (Maximum take-off): 18,960kg (41,800lb)
Dimensions: Length: 16.3m (53ft 6in), Wingspan: 20.6m (67ft 7in), Height: 4.98m (16ft 4in)
Powerplant: Two 1268kW (1700hp) Wright R-2600-13 Twin Cyclone 14-cylinder air-cooled radial piston engines
Maximum speed: 442km/h (275mph)
Range: 4350km (2700 miles)
Ceiling: 7255m (23,800ft)
Crew: 7
Armament: 'Solid' nose version: Eight 12.7mm (0.5in) Browning M2 fixed forward-firing machine guns in the nose; two 12.7mm (0.5in) Browning M2 fixed forward-firing machine guns in blisters on each side of the forward fuselage, two 12.7mm (0.5in) Browning M2 machine guns in dorsal turret, two 12.7mm (0.5in) machine guns flexibly mounted in waist position, two 12.7mm (0.5in) machine guns flexibly mounted in tail turret; up to 1814kg (4000lb) bomb load

12.7mm (0.5in) machine guns, resulting in a less specialized strafing platform. Later production B-25Hs added four further 12.7mm (0.5in) guns in blisters on the fuselage sides. In addition, both B-25G and H also retained the ability to carry a bomb load.

B-25J
The final B-25 production model, the B-25J, saw a return to the glazed bombardier nose, though it was still provided with a very heavy forward-firing armament, retaining the four machine gun blisters on the fuselage sides. Some production blocks were fitted with a solid nose equipped with eight 12.7mm (0.5in) machine guns. With its maximum armament of eighteen guns, the solid-nosed B-25J was the most heavily armed attack aircraft in the Allied arsenal. The aircraft also retained the deepened rear fuselage with rear gun position and flexible waist guns in the rear fuselage. First flown in October 1943, the B-25J

would be built in the largest numbers of any variant, with 4318 rolling off the Kansas City production line, Inglewood by this time having switched exclusively to P-51 Mustang production. Most B-25Js re-equipped existing B-25 units, but production shortages meant that some squadrons did not receive the new aircraft until late 1944. 316 B-25Js went to the RAF as the Mitchell III.

In addition to the USAAF and RAF, substantial use of the Mitchell was made by the Soviet Union, which received 823 aircraft and used them in the ADD – the Long Range Aviation Arm – for conventional bombing of strategic targets. The Soviet Union retained many after the war, leading to the Mitchell receiving the NATO reporting name 'Bank'.

PBJ-1
The US Navy also used a significant number of B-25s as the PBJ-1, which were operated nearly exclusively by the Marine Corps as land-based bombers

North American PBJ-1H
Weight (Maximum take-off): 15,876kg (35,000lb)
Dimensions: Length: 15.49m (50ft 10in), Wingspan: 20.6m (67ft 7in), Height: 4.98m (16ft 4in)
Powerplant: Two 1268kW (1700hp) Wright R-2600-13 Twin Cyclone fourteen-cylinder air-cooled radial piston engines
Maximum speed: 441km/h (275mph)
Range: 2173km (1350 miles)
Ceiling: 7560m (24,800ft)
Crew: 5
Armament: One 75mm T13E1 cannon fixed forward-firing in nose, four 12.7mm (0.5in) Browning M2 machine guns fixed forward-firing in nose, two 12.7mm (0.5in) M2 machine guns fixed forward-firing in blisters on starboard fuselage side, two 12.7mm (0.5in) Browning M2 machine guns in dorsal turret, two 12.7mm (0.5in) machine guns flexibly mounted in waist position, two 12.7mm (0.5in) machine guns flexibly mounted in tail; up to 1450kg (3200lb) bomb load

from March 1944. These bombers primarily operated on long-range interdiction missions against Japanese shipping, though nocturnal raids using the 298mm (11.75in) Tiny Tim rocket were briefly flown against the Japanese mainland from Iwo Jima in the period between the second atomic bomb attack and the final Japanese surrender.

Other wartime users included France, the Netherlands, Australia and China. Postwar, the aircraft saw widespread service, proving

North American PBJ-1H
This aircraft is from the USMC's 614th Marine Bomber Squadron (VMB-614), based on Hawaii, 1945. The type was modified with the eight-gun nose for low altitude strafing missions.

Solid-nosed B-25Js carried a battery of eight nose-mounted 12.7mm (0.5in) machine guns with 3200 rounds of ammunition. These aircraft were photographed on Iwo Jima during June 1945.

particularly popular in Latin America, though the last operational B-25s in service anywhere were finally retired by Indonesia in 1979.

Extremely popular in service due to its easy handling characteristics, combat effectiveness and dependability, the only significant complaint from B-25 crews stemmed from its extremely loud flight deck; the exhaust arrangement happened to direct all the engine noise at the cockpit, and many Mitchell crew suffered from hearing loss as a result.

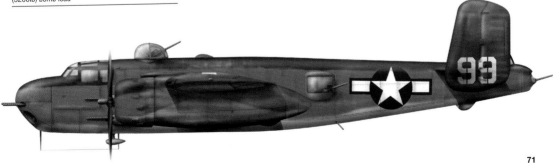

North American B-25H Mitchell

CUTAWAY KEY

1 Nose machine-gun barrels
2 Hinged nose compartment access door
3 Four 12.7mm (0.5in) machine-guns
4 Ammunition feed chutes
5 Cannon muzzle aperture
6 Nosewheel steering control
7 Aft-retracting nosewheel
8 Torque scissor links
9 Aerial mast
10 Nosewheel leg pivot mounting
11 Cannon barrel
12 Ammunition feed chutes
13 Machine-gun ammunition magazines, 400 rpg
14 Fixed bead sight
15 Armoured bulkhead
16 Windscreen panels
17 Instrument panel shroud
18 Pilot's gunsight
19 Direct vision opening window panel
20 Windscreen de-misting air ducts
21 Instrument panel
22 Control column
23 Rudder pedals
24 Cockpit armoured skin-plating
25 T13E1 75mm cannon
26 Recoil mechanism
27 Cannon mounting subframe
28 D/F loop aerial
29 HF aerial cable
30 Extending boarding ladder
31 Forward entry hatch
32 Machine-gun blister fairing
33 75mm cannon loading trough, hand-loaded shells
34 Shell case collector
35 12.7mm (0.5in) fixed machine-guns
36 Ammunition magazines
37 Ammunition feed chutes

38 Fire extinguisher bottle
39 Armoured seat backs
40 Pilot's seat
41 Safety harness
42 Sliding side-window panel
43 Navigator/radio operator/cannoneer's seat
44 Armoured headrests
45 Cockpit roof ditching hatch
46 Flight engineer/dorsal gunner's station
47 Cockpit bulkhead
48 Radio equipment racks
49 75mm cannon shell magazines, 21 rounds
50 Turret control foot pedals
51 Cabin heating air duct
52 Fresh air intake
53 Inner wing panel engine pylon mounting front spar
54 Cabin heater unit
55 Hydraulic reservoir
56 Wing panel centre-section carry-through
57 Turret gun ammunition magazines
58 Turret mounting ring
59 Forward/centre fuselage joint frame
60 Twin 12.7mm (0.5in) machine-guns
61 Bendix power-operated dorsal gun turret
62 Starboard inner wing pane
63 Nacelle top fairings
64 Cowling air flaps
65 Ejector type exhaust ducts
66 Detachable engine cowlings
67 Starboard Hamilton Standard constant-speed three-bladed propeller
68 Carburettor air intake
69 Outboard auxiliary fuel tank
70 Starboard oil coolers
71 Oil cooler air intake

72 Starboard landing lamp
73 12.7mm (0.5in) HVAR rockets
74 Pitot head
75 Starboard navigation light
76 Aileron balance weights
77 Starboard fabric-covered aileron
78 Aileron tab
79 Aileron operating linkage
80 Starboard outboard slotted flap
81 Oil cooler air outlets
82 Nacelle tail fairing
83 Starboard inboard slotted flap
84 Gun deflectors (tailplane protection)
85 Bomb bay roof crawlway
86 Bomb-hoisting frame
87 Vertical bomb rack
88 Port bomb stowage, maximum bombload 1360kg (3,00lb)
89 Gun turret motor amplidyne
90 Centre/rear fuselage joint frame
91 Rear fuselage heater unit
92 Starboard 12.7mm (0.5in) waist machine-gun
93 Dinghy stowage
94 Dinghy hatch
95 Fuselage skin panelling
96 Ammunition feed chutes
97 Starboard waist gun ammunition box
98 Starboard tailgun ammunition box
99 Tailgun feed chute
100 Tailplane centre section
101 Tailplane rib and spar construction
102 Starboard tailfin
103 HF aerial cable
104 Fabric-covered rudder
105 Rudder horn balance
106 Rudder tab
107 Fabric-covered elevator construction
108 Elevator tab

109 Tail gunner's seat
110 Head armour
111 Rearward armoured panel
112 Tail barbette
113 Twin 12.7mm (0.5in) machine-guns
114 Elevator tab
115 Port elevator
116 Port rudder rib construction
117 Rudder tab
118 Fin rib construction
119 Fin/tailplane attachment joint
120 Port tailplane
121 Tail gunner's seat
122 Tail compartment access
123 Rear fuselage/ tailplane joint frame
124 Tail bumper
125 Fuselage frame construction
126 Port tail gun ammunition box
127 Port waist gun ammunition box
128 Air scoop
129 Fuselage walkway
130 Emergency stores pack
131 Rear entry hatchway
132 Extending boarding ladder
133 Gun pintle mounting
134 Flexible canvas seal
135 Port waist gun cupola
136 Port 12.7mm (0.5in) waist machine-gun
137 Cartridge case collector
138 Port inboard slotted flap segment
139 Flap rib construction
140 Emergency stores pack
141 Inner wing rear spar
142 Fuselage/wing skin joint strap
143 Rear main fuel tank, 164 US gal (621 litres)
144 Forward main fuel tank, 572 litres (151 US gal)
145 Auxiliary fuel tanks, 575 litres (152 US gal) in three fuel cells per wing
146 Flap actuator links
147 Flap hydraulic jack

148 Port oil coolers
149 Oil cooler exhaust ducts
150 Nacelle tail fairing
151 Port outer-slotted flap segment
152 Outer wing panel rib construction
153 Aileron spar
154 Aileron tab
155 Port aileron rib construction
156 Aileron spar
157 Wingtip rib construction
158 Port navigation light
159 Outerwing panel leading edge ribs
160 Main spar
161 12.7mm (0.5in) HVAR rockets
162 Port landing lamp
163 Mainwheel doors
164 Main undercarriage wheel bay
165 Outer wing panel joint rib
166 Mainwheel hydraulic retraction jack
167 Nacelle auxiliary fuel tank
168 Mainwheel mounting subframe
169 Oil cooler air intake
170 Mainwheel shock absorber leg strut
171 Mainwheel leg door
172 Port mainwheel
173 Torque scissor links
174 Engine mounting subframe
175 Battery stowage
176 Engine bay firewall
177 Engine bearer struts
178 Accessory equipment bay
179 Cowling air flaps
180 Wright R-2600-13 14-cylinder two-row radial engine
181 Carburettor air intake
182 Detachable cowling panels
183 Propeller reduction gearbox
184 Propeller hub pitch change mechanism
185 Cowling nose ring/ cooling air intake
186 Port three-bladed propeller
187 907kg (2,000lb) torpedo

This B-25H Mitchell was armed with a 75mm T13E1 cannon for the ground attack role.

SPECIFICATION
NORTH AMERICAN B-25H MITCHELL

Crew
Five (one pilot, navigator/bombardier, turret gunner/engineer, radio operator/waist gunner, tail gunner)

Powerplant
Two 1268kW (1700hp) Wright R-2600-13 14-cylinder air-cooled radial engines

Performance:
Maximum speed: 443km/h (275mph) at 3960m (13,000ft); Climb to 4570m (15,000ft) in 19 min; Service ceiling: 7255m (23,800ft); Normal range: 2173km (1350 miles)

Weights
Empty: 9061kg (19,975lb); Maximum take-off: 16,351kg (36,047lb)

Dimensions
Wingspan: 20.60m (67ft 7in); Length: 15.54m (51ft)
Height: 4.80m (15ft 9in); Wing area: 56.67m² (610 sq ft)

Armament
One 75mm T13E1 gun with 21 shells in nose, four 12.7mm (0.5in) machine-guns in extreme nose, four in 'blisters' on side of nose, two in dorsal turret, two in extreme tail and one in each waist position of rear fuselage, plus up to eight 127mm (5in) rocket projectiles under the outer wings and up to 1361kg (3,000lb) of bombs carried internally

Martin B-26 Marauder

The Marauder was an advanced design that weathered a difficult service introduction to become the USAAF's premier tactical bomber in Europe.

Like its contemporary, the B-25 Mitchell, the Marauder was ordered 'off the drawing board' after Martin submitted its Model 179 design in response to the March 1939 USAAC Circular Proposal 39-640, calling for a twin-engined medium bomber with a maximum speed of 560km/h (350mph), a range of 4800km (3000 miles) and a bomb load of 910kg (2000lb). This was a challenging specification, and the Martin design team, led by Project Engineer Peyton M. Magruder (then only 27 years old), responded with an aerodynamically advanced design that featured a tricycle undercarriage and a notably small wing. This resulted in an aircraft with the highest wing loading yet accepted by the USAAC.

Contract issued

The Model 179 was judged the best of the competing proposals, with the B-25 in second place, and a contract for 201 production aircraft, designated B-26, was issued on 10 September 1939. No XB-26 prototype was built, and the first example was flown on 25

November 1940, with test pilot William K. Ebel at the controls.

By the time of its first flight, the Air Corps had ordered a further 179 B-26As with self-sealing fuel tanks as well as 719 B-26Bs with further improvements, bringing the total on order to 1131 – a huge total, given the aircraft had not yet been flown. Initial flight testing passed with no major incidents, and deliveries began in February 1941.

First use

The first unit to equip on the B-26 was the 22nd Bombardment Group (Medium) based at Langley Field, Virginia, which had previously operated Douglas B-18s. Initial service use was curtailed by a series of nose wheel collapses that were eventually cured by adjusting the centre of gravity of the aircraft and some localized strengthening. By October, the externally identical B-26A was beginning to be delivered. It could carry a torpedo if required and also featured a ferry tank in the rear bomb

bay and an upgraded electrical system as well as self-sealing fuel tanks. In the same month, after considering the somewhat bizarre alternative name of 'Martian', the official name of 'Marauder' was assigned to the B-26.

Martin B-26

Weight (Maximum take-off): 14,526kg (32,025lb)
Dimensions: Length: 17.07m (56ft), Wingspan: 19.81m (65ft), Height: 6.05m (19ft 10in)
Powerplant: Two 1380kW (1850hp) Pratt & Whitney R-2800-5 Double Wasp air-cooled radial piston engines
Maximum speed: 507km/h (315mph)
Range: 1609km (1000 miles)
Ceiling: 7620m (25,000ft)
Crew: 5
Armament: One 7.62mm (0.3in) Browning M1919 machine gun flexibly mounted in nose, two 12.7mm (0.5in) Browning M2 machine guns in dorsal turret, one 7.62mm (0.3in) Browning M1919 machine gun flexibly mounted in ventral tunnel position, one 12.7mm (0.5in) Browning M2 machine gun flexibly mounted in tail position; up to 2631kg (5800lb) bombs

Martin B-26 Marauder

B-26-MA (serial no 40-1415), nicknamed 'Fury', flew with the 19th Bombardment Squadron, 22nd Bomb Group, based in New Guinea, January 1944. This aircraft was part of the 'Silver Fleet', the only combat unit in the area using natural metal finish on their aircraft.

Martin B-26B Marauder

B-26B-55 (serial no. 42-96152) was part of the 598th Bombardment Squadron, 397th Bomb Group, based at Dreux, France, in September 1944. The diagonal yellow stripe on the tailplane signifies the 397th BG.

This same name was adopted by the RAF when it took delivery of 55 B-26As as the Marauder Mk I. A redesign of the rear gun position to mount two 12.7mm (0.5in) machine guns in place of the single weapon of earlier aircraft was the most obvious external change incorporated into the B-26B (Marauder IA in RAF service), destined to become the single most produced Marauder subtype, with 1883 built, though quite major design changes would be made in later B-26B production blocks.

B-26B

The B-26B first appeared in May 1942, by which time the Marauder had made its debut in combat operations. Following Pearl Harbor, the 22nd BG had moved overseas via Hawaii and Australia to the South West Pacific Area (SWPA) of operations, flying their first bombing mission against the Japanese base at Rabaul on 5 April 1942. Over the course of further operations against Rabaul and other targets, the Marauders generally flew unescorted and gave a good account of themselves in the face of strong Japanese fighter defences.

During the Battle of Midway in June, the B-26 made its debut as a torpedo bomber. Four Marauders were equipped with external torpedo racks

underneath the keel and attacked Japanese carriers. The torpedo runs began at an altitude of 244m (800ft), the B-26s then dropping down to only 3m (10ft) above the water under heavy attack from Japanese fighters. Two of the Marauders were lost in this action, and the other two were heavily damaged. No hits were made on the Japanese carriers, and the Marauder did not see further use in this role with US forces, though British and South African units would later successfully utilize the Marauder as a torpedo aircraft in the Mediterranean.

The B-26 quickly gained a reputation for high speed and ruggedness, proving superior in action to the B-25, as it could take greater punishment, was defensively superior and could fly faster with a heavier bomb load. However, as the Allies advanced in the South Pacific, the B-25, with its better short-field characteristics, good sortie rate and minimal maintenance requirements began to take over from the Marauder. It was decided therefore to adopt the B-25 as the standard medium bomber for the entire Pacific theatre and to use the B-26 exclusively in the Mediterranean and European theatres. The last B-26 sorties in the Pacific were flown on 9 January 1944.

Martin B-26B

Weight (Maximum take-off): 16,783kg (37,000lb)

Dimensions: Length: 17.75m (58ft 3in), Wingspan: 21.64m (71ft), Height: 6.05m (19ft 10in)

Powerplant: Two 1491kW (2000hp) Pratt & Whitney R-2800-43 Double Wasp air-cooled radial piston engines

Maximum speed: 454km/h (282mph)

Range: 1850km (1150 miles)

Ceiling: 6614m (21,700ft)

Crew: 7

Armament: One 12.7mm (0.5in) Browning M2 machine gun flexibly mounted in nose position, four 12.7mm (0.5in) Browning M2 machine gun fixed forward-firing in blisters on fuselage sides, two 12.7mm (0.5in) Browning M2 machine guns in dorsal turret, two 12.7mm (0.5in) Browning M2 machine guns in tail turret, two 12.7mm (0.5in) Browning M2 machine gun flexibly mounted in waist position; up to 1814kg (4000lb) bomb load

Mediterranean action

The Marauder first went into action over the Mediterranean with both British and US forces during November 1942, with Eighth Air Force operations from British bases following in May 1943. Over North Africa and the Mediterranean, the B-26 proved highly successful in bombing, long-range reconnaissance and anti-shipping operations. British squadrons also successfully used the aircraft as a heavy fighter, shooting down a considerable number of

Martin B-26B Marauder

This B-26B (serial no. 41-31173), nicknamed 'Flak Bait', was part of the 449th Bombardment Squadron, 322nd Bomb Group, based at Andrews Field Aerodrome, England, in 1944. 'Flak Bait' is well known for completing over 200 bombing missions over Europe and is preserved today at the Smithsonian Institution in Washington, D.C.

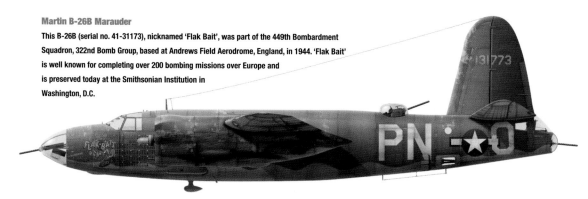

German and Italian transport aircraft flying between Italy and North Africa.

In service with the US 12th Air Force, the B-26 units suffered heavier losses than B-25 squadrons but achieved a great reputation for bombing accuracy, the B-26-equipped 42nd BG being described as "probably the best day-bomber unit in the world" by Deputy Commander-in-Chief Mediterranean Allied Air Forces Air Marshal John Slessor. Over Western Europe, the B-26 had a disastrous time when committed to low-level attack, losing 10 of 11 aircraft committed to its debut low-altitude mission. A subsequent switch to medium-level operations, and the transfer of the entire B-26 force from the Eighth to the Ninth Air Force, proved extremely successful, and the aircraft again garnered a reputation for great accuracy as well as achieving an astoundingly low loss rate of less than 0.5 per cent.

'PN' codes identify this B-26B as an aircraft of the 449th Bombardment Squadron, 322nd Bomb Group. The 322 BG was the first B-26 unit assigned to the European theatre.

The Widowmaker?

While the B-26 was being successfully committed to action overseas, it was simultaneously gaining a sinister reputation in the US due to a prohibitively high accident rate during training. This led to a swathe of derogatory nicknames, such as 'Martin Murderer', 'Flying Coffin', 'B-Dash-Crash' and the most popular: 'Widowmaker'. The regularity of crashes at MacDill Field led to the catchphrase, "One a day in Tampa Bay". This was an exaggeration but not a huge one – during one 30-day period, B-26 losses at MacDill averaged one every two days.

While this was clearly worrying, the accident rate was also puzzling, as between November 1940 and November 1941, only two fatal Marauder accidents had occurred, and operational squadrons were not experiencing anything like the same attrition. The problem, it transpired, had several causes.

The pressures of war had intensified training requirements, and although the B-26 was not an inherently dangerous aircraft, it did require precise handling, and both student pilots and indeed their instructors were not as experienced as pre-war service pilots. In addition, the ever-increasing amount of service equipment had inexorably pushed up weight with no increase in engine power, increasing the already high wing loading. A problem was found with the propellers, which were regularly running out of control and automatically feathering, an issue traced to poor maintenance from inexperienced ground crew. If this occurred on take-off, the drag of the feathered propeller regularly caused the aircraft to flip in the direction of the feathered prop, proving invariably fatal at low altitude.

The aircraft's problems were gradually overcome by improved training for both air and ground crew. However, until then, civilian ferry pilots regularly refused to fly the Marauder (on more than one occasion resigning from their position rather than do so), aircrew requested transfers to B-25 units and the B-26 was investigated by the US Senate on four occasions. Glenn L. Martin, the eponymous president of the company, was summoned to testify before the Senate Special Committee to Investigate the National Defense Program, popularly known as the Truman Committee,

which was investigating defence contracting abuses. The committee twice recommended that Marauder production be stopped, but the successful lowering of the training accident rate and the good opinion of aircrew in the field saw B-26 production escape termination. The USAAF had appointed General James Doolittle (of Doolittle Raid fame) to investigate the

Martin B-26C

Weight (Maximum take-off): 16,783kg (37,000lb)
Dimensions: Length: 17.75m (58ft 3in), Wingspan: 21.64m (71ft), Height: 6.05m (19ft 10in)
Powerplant: Two 1491kW (2000hp) Pratt & Whitney R-2800-43 Double Wasp air-cooled radial piston engines
Maximum speed: 454km/h (282mph)
Range: 1850km (1150 miles)
Ceiling: 6614m (21,700ft)
Crew: 7
Armament: One 12.7mm (0.5in) Browning M2 machine gun flexibly mounted in nose position, four 12.7mm (0.5in) Browning M2 machine gun fixed forward-firing in blisters on fuselage sides, two 12.7mm (0.5in) Browning M2 machine guns in dorsal turret, two 12.7mm (0.5in) Browning M2 machine guns in tail turret, two 12.7mm (0.5in) Browning M2 machine gun flexibly mounted in waist position; up to 1814kg (4000lb) bomb load

Martin B-26C Marauder
This B-26C-45-MO Marauder (42-107812/KS-J), nicknamed 'Baby Bumps II', was part of the 557th Bombardment Squadron, 387th Bomber Group, circa 1944.

problem. He found nothing intrinsically wrong with the aircraft, demonstrating his finding in spectacular style by carrying out some demonstration flights in which he cut an engine on take-off, rolled the B-26 onto its back, flew the plane upside down at an extremely low altitude for a distance and then righted it safely. At the time, it was widely believed that the B-26 could not be flown on one engine. Further flight demonstrations were made at training units to demonstrate how the aircraft might be recovered from unusual flight attitudes, and Doolittle's technical assistant Captain Vincent W. 'Squeak' Burnett made numerous demonstration flights with one engine out. In 1944, Martin even combined with the USAAF on a series of articles in various popular publications to educate the public and defend the flying record of the B-26 against 'slanders'.

Despite this gargantuan effort, and the fact that the B-26 enjoyed the lowest loss rate of any US combat aircraft flying in Europe, the Marauder's reputation never entirely recovered, and many trainee pilots still believed that the aircraft was a deathtrap. Some pilots still refused to fly the B-26 and had to be reassigned to other units.

Redesign

One change that did occur as a result of the investigations into the poor accident rate of the Marauder was a redesign of the wing, increasing the span and reducing wing loading. Despite decreasing the maximum speed slightly, the new wing led to a considerably shortened take-off distance. This change was incorporated into B-26B production and required that the vertical tail be increased in height to maintain stability with this larger wing. The benefit of the new wing was negated somewhat by the increase in gross weight of the aircraft due to the addition of ever-greater gun armament. This was the result of combat experience, with four forward-firing 12.7mm (0.5in) 'package' guns mounted on the fuselage sides in blisters added to the already heavy defensive armament (12 machine guns were carried in total).

The new wing was also incorporated in the B-26C variant, which was basically identical to the B-26B albeit built at a new plant in Omaha, Nebraska. Of the 1210 B-26Cs built, 123 went to the RAF as the Marauder II, passing most of them on to South African units supporting

operations in Italy. Both the B-26D and B-26E designations were issued to experimental conversions – a lightened variant and a variant with a different de-icing system, respectively – that did not enter production.

The B-26F, however, introduced a further change to the wing in that its

angle of incidence was increased by 3.5 degrees in a bid to further improve the take-off run and lower landing speed. Only 300 were built; 200 of these were supplied to the RAF as the Marauder Mk III, equipping two British and five South African squadrons.

By contrast, 893 of the similar B-26G were produced, which differed from the B-26F only in its usage of universal Army/Navy equipment rather than Air Force equipment. This variant

Martin B-26C Marauder

B-26C-45-MO (serial no. 42-107666), nicknamed 'Barracuda', flew with the 495th Bombardment Squadron, 344th Bomb Group, based at RAF Stansted Mountfitchet, England. 'Barracuda' is seen here painted with D-Day invasion stripes during June 1944.

Martin B-26C Marauder

B-26C-45-MO (serial no. 42-107542), named 'Mary Ann', was part of the 434th Bombardment Squadron, 344th Bomb Group, flying from AAF Station 169, Stansted, Essex, England, in early 1944. The 11 12.7mm (0.5in) M2 Browning machine guns are obvious from this profile view: one flexible in the nose position, four fixed in blisters on the fuselage (fired by the pilot), two in the dorsal turret, two in the tail turret, and one each in port and starboard lower waist positions.

Martin B-26C

Weight (Maximum take-off): 16,783kg (37,000lb)

Dimensions: Length: 17.75m (58ft 3in), Wingspan: 21.64m (71ft), Height: 6.05m (19ft 10in)

Powerplant: Two 1491kW (2000hp) Pratt & Whitney R-2800-43 Double Wasp air-cooled radial piston engines

Maximum speed: 454km/h (282mph)

Range: 1850km (1150 miles)

Ceiling: 6614m (21,700ft)

Crew: 7

Armament: One 12.7mm (0.5in) Browning M2 machine gun flexibly mounted in nose position, four 12.7mm (0.5in) Browning M2 machine gun fixed forward-firing in blisters on fuselage sides, two 12.7mm (0.5in) Browning M2 machine guns in dorsal turret, two 12.7mm (0.5in) Browning M2 machine guns in tail turret, two 12.7mm (0.5in) Browning M2 machine gun flexibly mounted in waist position; up to 1814kg (4000lb) bomb load

was also designated Marauder III when used by British Commonwealth forces. The last B-26G was delivered by Martin on 18 April 1945, bringing Marauder production to an end after a total of 5288 had been built.

As well as seeing combat service with US, British and South African forces, the Marauder was also supplied in some numbers to Free French units from late 1943 onwards. Initially supplied with early model war-weary ex-USAAF aircraft, the six French units so equipped later received newer models, seeing much service in Italy and in the invasion of southern France.

Target tug

Although its primary role was as a medium bomber, the Marauder was also used in large numbers as a target

tug. The 203 B-26Bs and 350 B-26Cs converted to become AT-23A and AT-23B tugs respectively were used to tow targets at high altitude to train gunners. This aircraft was utilized for the same purpose by the US Navy, which designated it the JM-1. Fifty-seven B-26Gs were also converted for target tug duties to become the TB-26G, all but 10 of which were transferred to the Navy to become the JM-2. One B-26 was modified with a set of tandem mainwheels, with wing-mounted stabilizing wheels, in support of the Martin XB-48 and Boeing XB-47 programmes. Officially designated the XB-26H, the aircraft was colloquially known as the 'Middle River Stump Jumper' and carried out flight tests during May and June of 1945. Following the end of hostilities,

the B-26 left US service fairly quickly and, unlike its great rival, the B-25, saw no postwar service with foreign operators once withdrawn from British Commonwealth and French service due to its demanding reputation, though a handful were converted as high-speed corporate transports in the late 1940s.

NAVAL BOMBERS

The bombing aircraft of the US Navy were primarily developed to destroy an enemy fleet by dive bombing and torpedo attack. Although the SBD Dauntless, SB2C Helldiver and TBM Avenger would prove decisive at battles such as Midway and Coral Sea, by 1945 it was clear that the more versatile single seater, such as the AD-1 Skyraider, was where the future lay.

- Curtiss SBC Helldiver
- Northrop BT-1
- Brewster SB2A Buccaneer
- Vought SB2U Vindicator
- Douglas SBD Dauntless
- Lockheed A-28/A-29 Hudson
- Lockheed PV-1 Ventura
- Grumman TBF Avenger
- Curtiss SB2C Helldiver
- Douglas TBD Devastator
- Douglas AD-1 Skyraider
- Consolidated TBY Sea Wolf
- Martin AM-1 Mauler

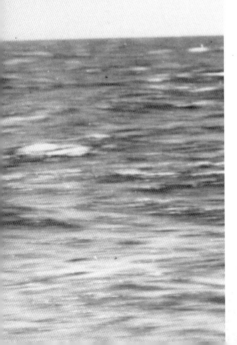

A US Navy Douglas TBD-1 Devastator (BuNo 0325, 6-T-4) of Torpedo Squadron 6 (VT-6) from the aircraft carrier USS *Enterprise* (CV-6) makes a practice drop with a Mark 13 torpedo on 20 October 1941.

Curtiss SBC Helldiver

Despite being developed as a monoplane, the Helldiver went into service as a biplane – the last that would be acquired by the US Navy.

Development of the Helldiver began in 1932, with a Navy requirement for a carrier-based fighter. Curtiss put forward their Model 73, which was powered by a Wright 1510-92 engine. It was a monoplane with high-mounted parasol wings and a retractable undercarriage. By the time a prototype was available, the requirement had evolved, first for a scout designated XS4C-1 and then for a scout bomber designated XSBC-1.

Adaptation and reinvention

The Model 73 was given an improved engine – a Wright R1820 Cyclone – and began testing. However, simulated dive-bombing was too much for the parasol wing, which was seriously

Curtiss SBC-4

This SBC-4 (BuAer No. 1287) served as a command liaison and transport aircraft with the 1st Marine Aviation Wing, San Diego, 1941. In conformity with the order of 30 December 1940 applying to all shipboard aircraft, the plane is painted in a light grey finish.

damaged in September 1934. The solution was to reinvent the Model 73 as a biplane, adding a lower pair of wings. This greatly improved the ruggedness of the overall wing assembly. Designated Model 77 by Curtiss, the new variant was upgraded to Model 77A status by the replacement of its engine with a Pratt & Whitney R-1535-82 Twin Wasp Junior. This version was accepted by the US Navy as the SBC-3 Helldiver.

At this time, 83 SBC-3s were ordered, to be followed by 124 improved SBC-4 models. The first batch, delivered in July 1937, went to the VT-5 aboard USS *Yorktown*. USS *Enterprise* and USS *Saratoga* were equipped with SBC-3s as they became available, with USS *Lexington* receiving SBC-4s. Some 50 of the US Navy's SBC-4s were redirected to France to outfit the carrier Bearn. These received an upgraded armament, with the 7.62mm (0.3in) machine guns – one mounted fixed forward and one in a rear-of-cockpit mounting –

replaced with 12.7mm (0.5in) calibre weapons. Most of these aircraft met a disappointing fate. They were aboard Bearn when France surrendered, and were unloaded at Martinique, where they rapidly deteriorated.

Despite being a well-behaved aircraft with few vices, the Helldiver was obsolete by the time it entered service. At the outbreak of World War II, it had

---

Curtiss SBC-4

Weight: (Maximum take-off) 7632kg (33,462lb)
Dimensions: Length: 8.58m (28ft 2in), Wingspan: 10.36m (34ft), Height: 3.18m (10ft 5in)
Powerplant: One 630kW (850hp) Wright R-1820-34 Cyclone 9-cylinder air-cooled radial piston engine
Speed: 377km/h (234mph)
Range: 652km (405 miles)
Ceiling: 7300m (24,000ft)
Crew: 2
Armament: One 7.62mm (0.3in) M1919 Browning machine gun fixed forward-firing in nose, one 7.6mm (0.3in) M1919 Browning machine gun flexibly mounted in rear cockpit; up to 454kg (1000lb) bomb load

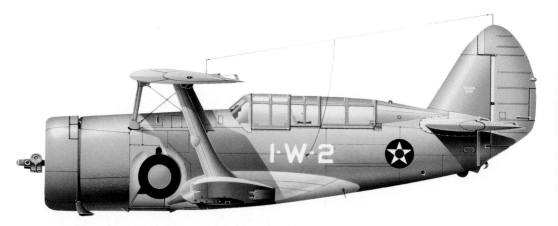

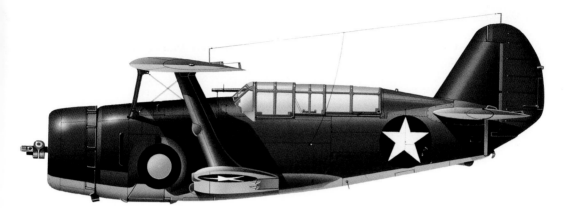

Curtiss SBC-3 Helldiver
This SBC-3 wears the post-May 1942 white star inside a blue roundel, in reserve squadron service. All upper surfaces are blue-grey and under surfaces were light grey.

been replaced aboard the US Navy's carriers by the Douglas Dauntless, though Marine Corps pilots continued to operate Helldivers as reconnaissance platforms until June 1943.

The withdrawn Helldivers became training aircraft, remaining in US service until October 1944. Other examples ended up in British hands by a convoluted route. Five examples intended for French service aboard Bearn were taken over by the British and used for training under the designation Cleveland I.

The SBC-3/4 Helldiver can be considered the last of its kind, or perhaps a transition model straddling the 'old' and 'new' worlds of maritime aviation. It began as a monoplane, evolving back into a biplane, and had relatively modern features including a metal fuselage and retractable undercarriage. With its relatively short range, weak armament and a top speed of 377km/h (234mph), it was greatly outclassed by the new generation of fighters it would have faced had it remained in service.

A Curtiss SBC-4 Helldiver assigned to US Marine Corps observation squadron VMO-151 undergoes flight testing.

Northrop BT-1

Although never fielded in great numbers, the BT-1 pioneered the use of air brakes to stabilize the aircraft in a dive.

The BT-1 was developed in response to a 1934 requirement for dive-bombers issued by the US Navy. Its designation can be confusing, as 'BT' may seem to imply a torpedo bomber. However, while the B does indeed stand for 'bomber', the T was a US Navy designation applied to aircraft built by Northrop. Fifty-four were delivered to the navy, entering service in 1938.

Oscillations of the tail

In theory, an aircraft diving directly at the target ought to be able to aim its bombs with precision. However, in practice, dive-bombers were prone to oscillations of the tail, known as buffeting, which introduced considerable variance in the aim point. Northrop's BT-1 offered a solution to this problem in the form of perforated flaps, greatly stabilizing the aircraft and improving bombing accuracy.

The bombing performance of the BT-1 was impressive, but the aircraft was underpowered and required some minor modifications before being accepted for service. The original 522kW (700hp) Pratt & Whitney XR-1535-66 engine was replaced with an improved version – a 615kW (825hp) R-1535-94 engine offering a top speed of 341km/h (212mph).

By the time it saw action in 1942, the BT-1 was already obsolete and had demonstrated serious flaws, including a poor rate of climb and a lack of slow-speed stability that resulted in several crashes. An improved version, designated XBT-2, was under development when Douglas took over Northrop in 1937.

Northrop BT-1

Weight (maximum take-off): 3271kg (7197lb)
Dimensions: Length: 9.65m (31ft 8in), Wingspan: 12.65m (41ft 6in), Height: 3.02m (9ft 11in)
Powerplant: One 615kW (825hp) Pratt & Whitney R-1535-94 Twin Wasp Jr. double row radial air-cooled engine
Maximum Speed: 357km/h (222mph)
Range: 1852km (1150 mi)
Ceiling: 7710m (25,300ft)
Crew: 2
Armament: 01 One 12.7mm (.50in) machine gun, one 7.62mm (.30in) machine gun; 454kg (1000lb) bomb under fuselage

Northrop BT-1
A US Navy Northrop BT-1 of dive-bomber squadron VB-5, assigned to the aircraft carrier USS *Yorktown* (CV-5). Deliveries of the BT-1 began in April 1938.

Brewster SB2A Buccaneer

Despite being wholly unsuitable for its role, the Buccaneer still managed to attract significant overseas orders. It never saw action, with some examples scrapped without ever being removed from their transport crates.

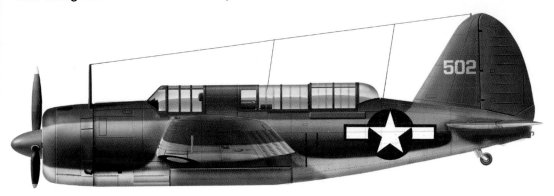

First flight was in June 1941, revealing a host of problems with the design. Redevelopment resulted in deletion of the intended turret in favour of a rear-of-cockpit mount for defensive armament and a slight lengthening of the fuselage. The addition of protection for the crew and self-sealing fuel tanks resulted in significant increases to the weight of an already underpowered aircraft.

The Buccaneer was in full-scale production before the first example flew, largely due to considerable overseas orders. France ordered 192 examples with an option for another 258 but was overrun before any deliveries took place. Britain took over this order and increased it to 750. An additional Dutch order for 192 aircraft was nullified by the collapse of Allied resistance in the Far East. These aircraft went to Britain and the USA.

The British Bermuda

Designated the Bermuda in British service, the Buccaneer proved immediately unsuccessful when it

Brewster SB2A-3 Buccaneer

This US Navy Buccaneer was utilized in the advanced training role, a task at which it functioned adequately, being of similar performance to the types that aircrews would take into action.

arrived in July 1942. Simultaneously too heavy and not tough enough for its intended role, the Buccaneer was underpowered and lacked the necessary manoeuvrability. The RAF quickly decided not to send crews into action in such a vulnerable machine, relegating the 206 it eventually received to a support role. RAF Bermudas served as trainers and target tugs.

The USAAF received 108 Buccaneers, which it designated A-34. These, too, were deemed unsuitable for any role more taxing than towing a target and were discarded by the end of 1944. The US Navy apparently thought a little better of its new aircraft, proclaiming the Buccaneer as satisfactory for carrier operations. The USN stopped short

Brewster SB2A-4

Weight: (Maximum take-off) 6481kg (14,289lb)

Dimensions: Length: 11.94m (39ft 2in), Wingspan: 14.33m (47ft), Height: 4.7m (15ft 5in)

Powerplant: One 1268kW (1700hp) Wright R-2600 Twin Cyclone 14-cylinder air-cooled radial piston engine

Speed: 441km/h (273mph)

Range: 2696km (1675 miles)

Ceiling: 7590m (24,900ft)

Crew: 2

Armament: Two 12.7mm (0.5in) M2 Browning machine guns fixed forward-firing in fuselage, two 7.62mm (0.3in) M1919 Browning machine guns fixed forward-firing in wings, two 7.62mm (0.3in) M1919 Browning machine guns flexibly mounted in rear cockpit, up to 226kg (500lb) bomb load in internal bomb bay and 226kg (500lb) bomb load on wing racks

of using the Buccaneer in combat, however, diverting its aircraft to the trainer role. Designated SB-2A, these proved useful, as they were similar to the more effective aircraft that crews would eventually take into action. The US Marine Corps formed night fighter squadrons with those it received.

Painful production

The Buccaneer was not only a failure as an aircraft; its entire history was fraught with problems. The Brewster company's performance has been described as shambolic; labour disputes were so bad that deliberate sabotage has been alleged. Long production delays resulted in an Australian order being cancelled, and later production was continued purely to keep the manufacturing process running until the switch-over to license-building Vought F4U Corsairs. This project was beset by the same labour difficulties and defective aircraft as the Buccaneer, leading to the demise of the Brewster Aeronautical Corporation in 1946.

Ultimately, 711 Buccaneers were built. None saw action, and many of the later aircraft were not even removed from their crates. Even as target tugs, they were considered as much a liability as an asset by some users and were phased out as soon as possible. Their only contribution to the war effort was sparing better aircraft from the trainer role, which hardly justifies the numbers built.

Vought SB2U Vindicator

The Vindicator was the first monoplane dive-bomber to enter US Navy service. It initially saw action in French hands, where it suffered heavy losses.

At the time the Vindicator was being developed, there was real doubt as to whether monoplanes were suitable for carrier operations. Accordingly, Vought constructed both a biplane (XSB3U-1) and a monoplane (XSB2U-1) prototype. The superior performance of the XSB2U-1 ensured it was the monoplane that was ordered, first flying in January 1936.

SB2U-1

Fifty-six of the original SB2U-1 Vindicator were constructed, to be followed by 58 of the SB2U-2 version. The SB2U-3, designed to be capable of using a wheeled undercarriage or floats, was intended mainly for Marine Corps use but ended up being the only variant to see action in US hands. Armament was typical for the time; a 12.7mm (0.5in) Browning machine gun on a flexible rear-of-cockpit mount and a second 12.7mm (0.5in) machine gun in a fixed-forward mounting in the starboard wing, with a 453kg (1000lb) bomb load.

European service

Although intended to operate from the carrier Bearn, French Vindicators flew from land bases during the defence of France. These aircraft were designated V 156-F and were basically SB2U-2s with some French equipment aboard. Attempting to slow the German advance, strikes were carried out against bridges as well as against troop concentrations, exposing the vulnerability of the design to more modern fighters.

Dunkirk evacuation

Nevertheless, despite heavy losses, the V 156-F proved useful in providing air support for the Dunkirk evacuation and subsequently transferred to a maritime strike role against Italian forces in the south.

It is thought that they may have sunk an Italian submarine before the Fall of France. Afterwards, Britain took over the V 156-Fs meant for France, intending to use them for anti-submarine work.

Referred to as the Chesapeake I in British service, the SB2U-2 was further modified to carry heavier armament and some armour. They also received the larger fuel tanks developed for the SB2U-3 version. However, these aircraft were underpowered and could not carry a sufficient payload. They went instead to a training role, with the anti-submarine task undertaken by Fairey Swordfish.

Losses at Midway

By the outbreak of World War II, the Vindicator had been replaced as a carrier-borne strike platform by the Douglas Dauntless. Some were present at Midway Island, in Marine Corps hands, when the Japanese attack began. Flown by VMSB-231, a mix of Vindicators and Dauntlesses counterattacked the Japanese fleet on 4–6 June.

These outdated aircraft suffered heavily from enemy anti-aircraft fire and fighter action, and 23 out of 30

Vought SB2U-2 Vindicator

An SB2U-2 of Scouting Squadron 42 (VS-42), serving aboard USS *Ranger*.

Vought SB2U-2 Vindicator

This aircraft was the 5th Section Leader of Bombing Squadron 2 (VB-2), deployed aboard USS *Lexington* in July 1939. Lemon yellow tail markings signified the *Lexington*.

Vought SB2U-2

Weight: (Maximum take-off) 4273kg (9421lb)

Dimensions: Length: 10.36m (34ft), Wingspan: 12.77m (41ft 11in), Height: 4.34m (14ft 3in)

Powerplant: One 615kW (825hp) Pratt & Whitney R-1535-02 Twin Wasp Junior 14-cylinder air-cooled radial piston engine

Speed: 391km/h (243mph)

Range: 1800km (1120 miles)

Ceiling: 7200m (23,600ft)

Crew: 2

Armament: One 12.7mm (0.5in) M2 Browning machine gun in starboard wing, one 12.7mm (0.5in) M2 Browning machine gun flexibly mounted in rear cockpit; up to 453kg (1000lb) bomb load under fuselage

were lost. The first Congressional Medal of Honour awarded to a Marine pilot during World War II was posthumously won by Captain Richard E. Fleming, whose SDB was damaged too badly to fly on 4 June. The next day, he volunteered to fly a Vindicator, pressing home an unsuccessful attack on the Japanese cruiser Mikuma even though his aircraft was in flames.

Douglas SBD Dauntless

The Douglas Dauntless was approaching obsolescence at the outbreak of World War II but proved to be a highly effective platform throughout the conflict.

Although the Northrop BT-1 solved some of the problems inherent in a naval dive-bomber, notably vertical oscillations of the tail during a dive, it was not a success.

Only 54 were built, with the US Navy soon seeking a higher-performance replacement. Northrop offered a developed version, designated BT-2, with a tidier retractable undercarriage and a more powerful engine. This was a Wright 1820 Cyclone, replacing the R-1535 Twin Wasp Junior of the BT-1.

'Slow but deadly'

First flight was in April 1938, by which time Northrop had been taken over by the Douglas Aircraft Company. Thus, the BT-2 was ordered for service with the US Navy and Marine Corps as the Douglas XSBD. The XSBD-2 model

ordered for the navy differed from the Marine XSBD-1 in that it had increased fuel capacity.

The SBD benefited from the dive brakes developed for the BT-1 but had much better low-speed manoeuvrability. Low speed became something of a hallmark, however, gaining the Dauntless the nickname 'slow but deadly'.

Nevertheless, it was used as a defensive fighter for carrier groups at times, for lack of higher-performance aircraft. Its two fixed forward-firing 12.7mm (0.5in) machine guns represented a rather basic armament for the role, but Dauntlesses were credited with some air-to-air kills.

In service

By the time the first Dauntlesses were delivered – to VB-2 aboard

Douglas A-24
Weight: (Maximum take-off) 4441kg (9790lb)
Dimensions: Length: 9.78m (32ft 1in), Wingspan: 12.66m (41ft 6in), Height: 4.14m (13ft 7in)
Powerplant: One 890kW (1200hp) Wright R-1820-60 Cyclone 9-cylinder air-cooled radial engine
Speed: 406km/h (253mph)
Range: 1875km (1165 miles)
Ceiling: 9022m (29,600ft)
Crew: 2
Armament: Two 12.7mm (0.5in) M2 Browning machine guns fixed forward-firing in cowling, one 7.62mm (0.30in) M1919 Browning machine gun flexibly mounted in rear cockpit; up to 544kg (1200lb) bomb load

Douglas A-24 Banshee

The Douglas A-24 Banshee was the US Army version of the US Navy SBD Dauntless dive-bomber with a few changes to suit the service. This plane served with the 312th Bomb Group, USAAF, based at Makin Island, 1943.

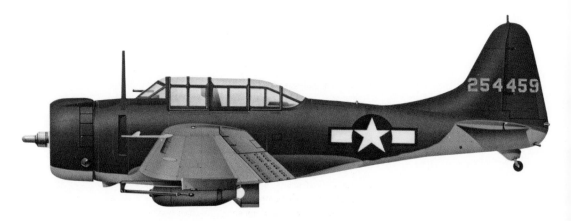

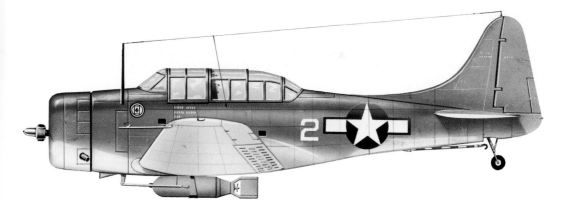

Douglas SBD-3 Dauntless

Weight: (Maximum take-off) 4699kg (10,360lb)

Dimensions: Length: 9.78m (32ft 1in), Wingspan: 12.66m (41ft 6in), Height: 4.14m (13ft 7in)

Powerplant: One 890kW (1200hp) Wright R-1820-60 Cyclone 9-cylinder air-cooled radial engine

Speed: 404km/h (251mph)

Range: 2220km (1380 miles)

Ceiling: 8310m (27,260ft)

Crew: 2

Armament: Two 12.7mm (0.5in) M2 Browning machine guns fixed forward-firing in cowling, two 7.62mm (0.30in) M1919 Browning machine guns flexibly mounted in rear cockpit; up to 544kg (1200lb) bomb load

USS *Lexington* and VB-6 aboard USS *Enterprise* – the Curtiss SB2U Helldiver was already flying. The Helldiver was intended to replace the Dauntless and not be in service for long. In reality, it continued to serve with distinction far longer than anticipated. The US Marine Corps, which received its Dauntlesses in late 1940 (before the US Navy), continued to operate them even after the Dauntless had been withdrawn from widespread naval service.

At the outbreak of World War II, about half of all US carrier aircraft were SBDs, and they saw action right from the very start. A flight of 18 Dauntlesses were en route to Hawaii from USS *Enterprise* when the Japanese attack on Pearl Harbor began. Seven were lost, but on 10 December 1941, SBDs from Enterprise sank submarine I-70. This marked the first Japanese vessel lost to air attack.

SBD-3s and SBD-4s

An improved variant, designated SBD-3, was developed from a French requirement specifying protective armour and self-sealing fuel tanks. Although France fell before any aircraft could be delivered, these

Douglas SBD-3 Dauntless

The SBD-3 had self-sealing fuel tanks and four machine guns. It could also carry a single 453kg (1000lb) general purpose bomb.

features were incorporated on US aircraft and greatly contributed to survivability. In total, 584 SBD-3s were built before production moved to the SBD-4 variant, which featured an improved rear-facing defensive weapons fit.

Pacific War

The SBD was vital to the Pacific war effort, especially against Japanese carrier forces at the Battle of Midway. Its final variant was the SBD-5, with a more powerful R-1820-60 Cyclone engine to offset the greater weight of equipment it was required to carry. 2965 SBD-5s were constructed, serving from the Pacific to the landings in North Africa to strikes against enemy ships in Norway.

The Dauntless suffered the lowest loss rate of all US Navy aircraft, but a version designated A-24 Banshee proved vulnerable in the hands of the USAAF, largely due to the practice of glide-bombing rather than dive-bombing.

Lockheed A-28/A-29 Hudson

Although the Hudson was little used by US forces, it was the first US aircraft to sink a U-boat and was operated in large numbers by the RAF and other air forces.

A military adaptation of the Lockheed Model 14 Super Electra airliner, the Hudson flew for the first time on 10 December 1938 and rapidly drew the attention of the British Purchasing Commission, which believed the aircraft would prove useful by supplementing the Avro Anson in the maritime patrol role. Two hundred were ordered, with the first being delivered during February 1939. A further 50 followed rapidly.

RAF maritime patrol role

Shortly after the outbreak of war, a Hudson became the first British-based aircraft to destroy an enemy aircraft when one managed to shoot down a Dornier Do 18 over Jutland, Denmark. Hudsons subsequently played a hugely important role as a maritime patrol aircraft in the RAF Coastal Command and are credited with sinking 21 U-boats and sharing in the destruction of a further five. In addition to their anti-submarine work, Hudsons were also utilized for reconnaissance flights over Germany and occupied Europe as well as clandestine operations in both Europe and Burma. Highlights of the Hudson's British career included the first sinking of an enemy submarine by rocket attack, and in August 1941, a Hudson bombed U-570, which then surrendered. This was the only instance of an enemy vessel surrendering to an Allied aircraft in World War II.

American service

Following America's entry into the war, many examples of the Hudson were requisitioned for US use and designated A-28 by the USAAF (or A-29 once production switched to more powerful engines).

The first 20 A-29s were issued to the US Navy, which called the Hudsons the PBO-1 and utilized them for maritime patrol. On 1 March 1942, a PBO-1 depth charged and sunk the submarine U-656 off Cape Race, Newfoundland. This was both the first U-boat to be sunk by the US Navy and the first sunk by an aircraft in US service. Hudsons would also be responsible for the first submarine sinkings achieved by both New Zealand and Brazil.

By the time production stopped in 1943, 2941 Hudsons had been built. Popular with crews and noted for its excellent reliability, the Hudson was nicknamed 'Old Boomerang' – because it always came back.

Lockheed A-29

Weight (Maximum take-off): 9662kg (21,300lb)
Dimensions: Length: 13.51m (44ft 4in), Wingspan: 19.96m (65ft 6in), Height: 3.62m (10ft 11in)
Powerplant: Two 895kW (1200hp) Wright R-1820-87 Cyclone nine cylinder air-cooled radial piston engines
Maximum speed: 407km/h (253mph)
Range: 2490km (1550 miles)
Ceiling: 8077m (26,500ft)
Crew: 5
Armament: Two 7.7mm (0.303in) Browning machine guns fixed forward-firing in the upper nose, two 7.7mm (0.303in) Browning machine guns in dorsal turret; up to 454kg (1000lb) bomb load

Lockheed A-29

This repossessed RAF Hudson III (BW454), serial number 41-23325, was used in anti-submarine patrols off the West Coast of the US, flying from Portland, Oregon, April 1942.

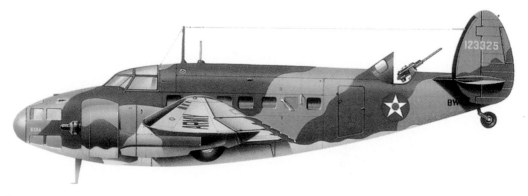

Lockheed PV-1 Ventura

Although it proved to be a disappointing medium bomber, the Ventura enjoyed a second lease of life as a maritime patrol aircraft, proving highly successful and remarkably versatile.

Derived from the Model 18 Lodestar airliner, the Ventura was proposed by Lockheed for British use as a replacement for both the Hudson and the Bristol Blenheim light bomber. In February 1940, an order was placed for 25 aircraft. This was quickly followed by contracts for 675 more.

Daylight raider

Delivered from mid-1942, Venturas were used for daylight RAF raids on occupied Europe, but they proved too vulnerable without fighter escort, which was not then possible for long-range missions. On one particularly disastrous raid, when 10 Venturas of 487 Squadron, Royal New Zealand Air Force (RNZAF) attacked a power station in Amsterdam, all were shot down. Replaced by the far superior de Havilland Mosquito, the Ventura was transferred to patrol duties with Coastal Command. There, it proved far more useful. Ultimately, Venturas would sink seven U-boats.

B-34 and PV-2

Two hundred and sixty-four of the Venturas ordered by the RAF were transferred to the USAAF, and some were used as anti-submarine patrol bombers under the designation B-34 Lexington, though most were used for training. In 1942, as part of a deal to secure the Naval plant at Renton for B-29 production, the US Navy obtained exclusive rights to the B-34 design and subsequently ordered a navalized variant designated the PV-1 Ventura, which entered service in February 1943. As well as maritime patrol, Navy Venturas undertook medium bombing missions against Japanese targets, and as one of the first radar-equipped land-based naval aircraft, often acted as a lead ship for liberator heavy bombers.

In the absence of any other more suitable aircraft, the PV-1 also became the Marine Corps' first dedicated night fighter and first radar-equipped aircraft, scoring its first victory in the early hours of 13 November 1943.

After being further developed into the PV-2 Harpoon, a fault with the wing required a major redesign, and only a few of this improved model saw service before the war's end.

Ventura variants saw a great deal of use post-war, with around a dozen nations (including for their previous foe, Japan). The aircraft's last user was Portugal, which retired the last of theirs in 1975. In total, 3028 examples of this aircraft were built.

PV-1 Ventura

Weight (Maximum take-off): 14,096kg (31,077lb)

Dimensions: Length: 15.8m (51ft 9in), Wingspan: 20m (65ft 6in)

Powerplant: Two 1,492 kw (2,000 hp) Pratt & Whitney R-2800-31 Double Wasp 18-cylinder air-cooled radial piston engines

Maximum speed: 502km/h (312mph)

Range: 2671km (1660 miles)

Ceiling: 8016m (26,300ft)

Crew: 6

Armament: Two 12.7mm (0.5in) fixed forward-firing Browning M2 machine guns in nose, 7.62mm (0.3in) Browning M1919 machine guns flexibly mounted in nose, two 7.62mm (0.3in) Browning M1919 machine guns in rear ventral position; two or four Browning M1919 machine guns in dorsal turret; up to 1134kg (2,500lb) bomb load

Lockheed PV-1 Ventura

This Ventura (no. 891) served with Patrol Bombing Squadron 135 (VB-135), US Navy, known as the 'Blind Foxes'. The squadron was based at Whidbey Island, Washington, and contributed to some of the earliest Allied victories in the Pacific theatre, including bombing Kiska Harbor in June 1942.

Grumman TBF Avenger

Despite its ungainly appearance, the Grumman TBF Avenger proved to be an excellent combat aircraft. It was instrumental in winning critical naval battles throughout the Pacific War.

The Avenger began development in 1939 in response to a requirement for a torpedo bomber capable of 483km/h (300mph) and with a range of 1609km (1000 miles). Ordnance was to be carried in an internal bay. The Grumman entry was one of 13 put forward, of which it and the Vought TBU were selected to be further developed. An order for 285 TBF-1 aircraft was placed in December 1940. A single TBF-2 was also ordered. Both variants used Wright engines: the TBF-1 used the R-2600-8, and the TBF-2, the R-2600-10.

Single-engine bruiser

The first prototype flew in August 1941. It was lost when the crew mistook oil mist from a leaking hydraulic pipe for smoke and abandoned the aircraft, but despite this setback, the second prototype passed testing with relatively minor changes requested. What emerged was the heaviest single-engined aircraft – and the largest to operate from a carrier – of the war. The amount of space required to stow it was reduced by using a compound angle folding wing mechanism.

Other unusual features of the Avenger included an electrically operated turret in the dorsal position mounting a 12.7mm (0.5in) machine gun. Rear defence was augmented by a 7.62mm (0.3in) machine gun in a flexible ventral rear mounting. A single 7.62mm (0.3in) machine gun in a fixed-forward mounting was replaced by a

pair of wing-mounted 12.7mm (0.5in) machine guns in the TBF-1C model.

The TBF was designated 'Avenger' by the US Navy in October 1941, and not in response to the Japanese attack on Pearl Harbor as was widely assumed at the time. Ultimately, 1524 TBF-1s were built by Grumman, with 550 more designated TBM-1s produced by General Motors. Four-hundred-and-two of the TBF-1B model

A TBF Avenger comes to a stop after making a qualification landing on a training escort carrier, circa 1943. At right, the plane director (in yellow cap and jersey) runs out to direct the pilot. Plane handlers and hook release men are running out from the catwalks.

were supplied to the Royal Navy, where they were initially known as the Tarpon. This was later changed to Avenger TR. Further models followed; the TBF-1C gained additional fuel and a modified forward armament. In total, 764 were produced by Grumman, and 2332 TBM-1s were delivered by General Motors. Variants carrying surface search radar, additional electronic equipment and other specialist systems appeared throughout the war.

Lessons learned in combat

The first TBF-1s were delivered aboard USS *Hornet* in April 1942, at a time when the US Navy was entirely dependent on its carriers for lack of serviceable battleships. Six Avengers from Torpedo Squadron 8 (VT-8) were unable to sail with Hornet when she departed for the Pacific, instead being transferred to Pearl Harbor and then Midway Island. They were present when news arrived of

the Japanese fleet approaching. The six Avengers, along with other aircraft, attempted to attack the enemy fleet. They were heavily outnumbered by fighters and faced effective shipboard anti-aircraft systems during their attack runs. Five TBF-1s were shot down, the sixth escaping with heavy damage. The Avenger force scored no hits on the Japanese force, though attacks later in the battle sank four carriers and a cruiser. Lessons learned from the surviving aircraft were incorporated in later development, leading to greater survivability. It was not until November 1942 that the Avenger finally sank an enemy warship: the battleship Hiei. Part of a powerful force sent to bombard the US airbase at Henderson Field on Guadalcanal, Hiei was damaged in a surface action and circling with her steering jammed. An attack by Avengers resulted in two torpedo hits, causing further damage. Facing continued air attack, and with no prospect of escape, the battleship was abandoned and sunk by her escorting destroyers.

The Grumman Avenger continued to serve with distinction throughout the

Grumman TBF-1 Avenger

Weight: (Maximum take-off) 8115kg (17895lb)

Dimensions: Length: 12.2m (40ft), Wingspan: 16.51m (54ft 2in), Height: 5m (16ft 5in)

Powerplant: One 1300kW (1700hp) Wright R-2600-8 Twin Cyclone 14-cylinder air-cooled radial piston engine

Speed: 447km/h (278mph)

Range: 1456km (905 miles)

Ceiling: 6900m (22600ft)

Crew: 3

Armament: One 7.62mm (0.3in) M1919 Browning machine gun fixed forward-firing in nose; one 12.7mm (0.5in) M2 Browning machine gun in rear turret, one 7.62mm (0.3in) M1919 Browning machine gun flexibly mounted in ventral position; up to 907kg (2000lb) bomb load or one 907kg (2000lb) Mark XIII torpedo or Mark 24 acoustic homing torpedo in bomb bay

Grumman TBF-1 Avenger

This TBF-1 was one of the first built by Grumman's Bethpage factory.

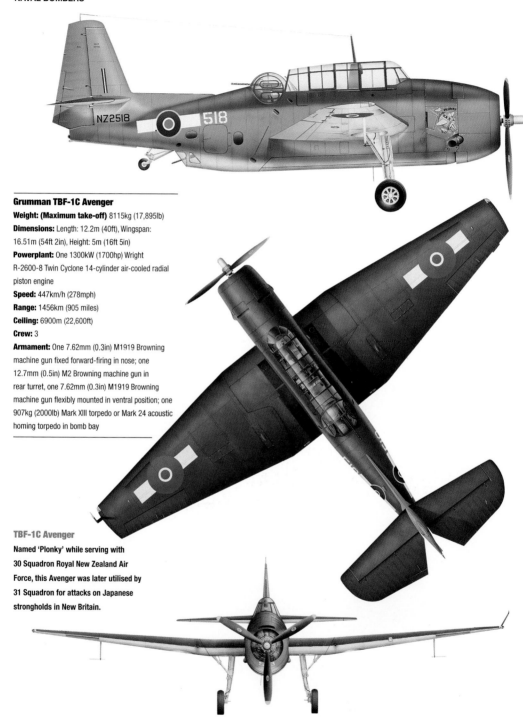

Grumman TBF-1C Avenger

Weight: (Maximum take-off) 8115kg (17,895lb)

Dimensions: Length: 12.2m (40ft), Wingspan:
16.51m (54ft 2in), Height: 5m (16ft 5in)

Powerplant: One 1300kW (1700hp) Wright
R-2600-8 Twin Cyclone 14-cylinder air-cooled radial
piston engine

Speed: 447km/h (278mph)

Range: 1456km (905 miles)

Ceiling: 6900m (22,600ft)

Crew: 3

Armament: One 7.62mm (0.3in) M1919 Browning
machine gun fixed forward-firing in nose; one
12.7mm (0.5in) M2 Browning machine gun in
rear turret, one 7.62mm (0.3in) M1919 Browning
machine gun flexibly mounted in ventral position; one
907kg (2000lb) Mark XIII torpedo or Mark 24 acoustic
homing torpedo in bomb bay

TBF-1C Avenger

Named 'Plonky' while serving with
30 Squadron Royal New Zealand Air
Force, this Avenger was later utilised by
31 Squadron for attacks on Japanese
strongholds in New Britain.

war, contributing to the sinking of the Japanese super battleships Musashi and Yamato. These heavily protected vessels withstood multiple torpedo and bomb hits, which gradually reduced their ability to manoeuvre, making later strikes more effective. Musashi is thought to have been struck by 19 torpedoes and 17 bombs, while Yamato suffered seven torpedo and 12 bomb hits. That the greatest battleships ever constructed were sunk by aircraft is an indicator of how rapidly air power came to dominate maritime warfare.

Other roles

One of the difficulties faced by Avenger pilots was the unreliability of their torpedoes. This was not confined to air-dropped weapons; submarine-launched torpedoes were also proving troublesome. In addition, torpedo attacks became increasingly dangerous as the war went on. Anti-aircraft armament

thought sufficient at the outbreak was greatly enhanced, and tactics for protecting high-value targets, such as carriers and battleships, were constantly developed. The steady, low approach of a torpedo aircraft made it particularly vulnerable to these defences.

As a result, Avengers moved into different roles as the war progressed. Alongside the torpedo strike mission, they served as scouts and light bombers in addition to supporting troops ashore. They made an important contribution in the Battle of the Atlantic, hunting submarines from shore stations and escort carriers. The primary anti-submarine weapon was the depth bomb, but later in the war rockets were developed for attacks on surfaced U-boats. Improvements in submarine anti-aircraft armament made this a hazardous undertaking, which was countered by cooperation with Wildcat fighters from the same

carrier. As the Wildcats strafed the submarine to suppress its flak, the Avengers were able to make their attack runs unopposed.

US carrier-based aircraft are credited with sinking or assisting in the sinking of 35 U-boats, and it is likely that Avengers were involved in all of these kills. Their payload capacity allowed flares and searchlights to be carried, greatly assisting in night searches, and some aircraft were fitted with surface search radar. The Avenger also carried the pioneering Mk 24 acoustic homing torpedo. Not only were these aircraft highly effective against the U-boats, but they also served as testbeds for anti-submarine techniques and remained in service for several years after the war.

A TBF-1 Avenger torpedo bomber drops a Mk XIII torpedo, 30 October 1942. This torpedo is fitted with a plywood tail shroud to improve its airborne performance.

Curtiss SB2C Helldiver

The SB2C Helldiver was plagued by problems in development and service entry, gaining a poor but largely undeserved reputation. It emerged as one of the most successful naval aircraft of the war.

By the time the Helldiver first flew in December 1940, 370 were already on order despite wind-tunnel tests that suggested serious problems with its handling. On paper, the design was very promising; it was faster and had greater range, with a more potent payload. However, testing demonstrated a host of problems. Over the next three years, some 880 design changes were made, some of them very significant.

The prototype's weaknesses occurred largely because of design constraints. A requirement that the aircraft be capable of passing through the deck lift of USS *Essex* meant that too much had to be crammed into a small airframe. The resulting aircraft was not rugged enough and had serious handling flaws including dangerous stall characteristics. The Wright R-2600 engine also caused problems.

Most of the Helldiver's handling problems stemmed from its proportions. Its wingspan was much greater than that of the Douglas Dauntless, made possible by using folding wings, but the fuselage could not be lengthened much and still meet the Navy's dimensions requirement. Thus, the Helldiver was only 71cm (2ft 4in) longer than the Dauntless and much heavier. Its tail section was too small to control the oscillations resulting from this configuration.

Poor impressions

The prototype crashed in February 1941 as a result of engine failure and was rebuilt with characteristics that would become its hallmark – a large tail, fin and rudder, which improved flying characteristics. However, this prototype was forced to crash-land in December 1941 after wing failure during dive tests, and it could not be rebuilt into flying condition. Additional changes, such as improved armament, added more weight and created another round of problems. The delays became so bad that the company was investigated by the Senate War Investigating Committee.

The first Helldivers, designated SB2C-1, were deemed unsuitable as combat aircraft and put into service as trainers, and it was the SB2C-3 variant that first saw combat in the hands of VB-17. Flying from USS *Bunker Hill*, Helldivers attacked Rabaul in November 1943. Despite a higher payload than the Dauntless it was intended to replace, the Helldiver was viewed unfavourably by its crews. It was faster but had a smaller operating radius and was not as stable a dive-bombing platform. A much heavier armament of two 20mm (0.79in) cannon in the wings

Curtiss SB2C-1C

The first production SB2Cs were fitted with two 12.7mm (0.50in) machine guns in each wing, but after 200 had been completed this was changed to a single 20mm (0.79in) cannon in each wing in the SB2C-1C.

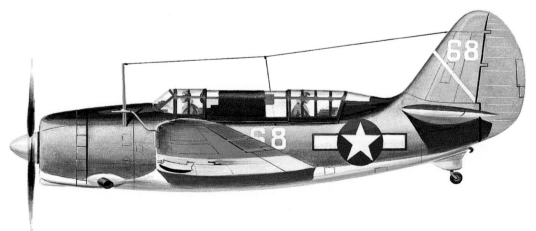

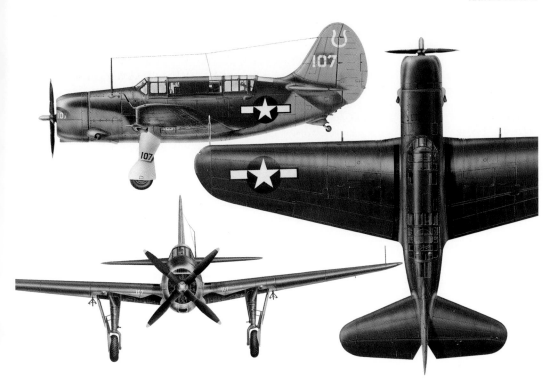

and a pair of 7.62mm (0.3in) Browning machine guns in a flexible rear mount did not offset unreliable electrical and hydraulic systems.

The Helldiver was called many uncomplimentary names, of which 'beast' was the mildest. Some decided that SB2C stood for 'Son of a bitch, second class'. Meanwhile, improvements struggled to keep up with the production schedule. The 601st aircraft to come off the production line was the first to incorporate all the design changes made along the way.

Meanwhile, overseas customers lost interest. Britain cancelled an order for 450, citing handling described as 'appalling', and the Royal Australian Air Force also cancelled its order for 150. The US Army Air Force had also shown interest in a variant of the Helldiver

designated A-25 Shrike, but changing requirements resulted in an order for 900 being cancelled. In total, 410 of these aircraft went to the Marine Corps.

SB2C-3

Ironically, the dive brakes fitted to improve bombing accuracy by reducing tail buffeting actually caused oscillations. Once this was realized and the brakes redesigned, the problem was largely overcome. Likewise, the installation of a more powerful R-2600-20 engine increased speed only a little but greatly reduced the aircraft's handling problems.

With these modifications, the SB2C-3 variant finally began to mature into an effective combat aircraft. It earned the respect of at least some of its crews but still retained its reputation as a serial underperformer.

Curtiss SB2C-3

Weight: (Maximum take-off) 7388kg (16,287lb)
Dimensions: Length: 11.18m (36ft 8in), Wingspan: 15.16m (49ft 9in), Height: 4.01m (13ft 2in)
Powerplant: One 1417kW (1900hp) Wright R-2600-20 Twin Cyclone 14-cylinder air-cooled radial piston engine
Speed: 475km/h (295mph)
Range: 1875km (1165 miles)
Ceiling: 8900m (29,100ft)
Crew: 2
Armament: Two 20mm (0.79in) AN/M2 cannon fixed forward-firing in wings, two 7.62mm (0.3in) M1919 Browning machine guns flexibly mounted in rear cockpit; up to 910kg (2000lb) bomb load or one 910kg (2000lb) Mark XIII torpedo in internal bomb bay, 452kg (1000lb) bomb load on wing racks

Replacement of Dauntlesses with Helldivers proceeded at a relatively leisurely pace, and some commanders believed that anything a Helldiver could do could be done better by another aircraft.

Battle of the Philippine Sea

By mid-1944, the Helldiver had developed into an effective combat platform, though it retained its poor reputation. US industrial might had created a much-enlarged carrier air arm, while the Japanese forces had lost most of their best pilots. They were still able to launch some 430 aircraft at the US fleet, which destroyed over 300 of them in what became known as the Great Marianas Turkey Shoot. More were lost later in

the battle, from which Japanese naval aviation never recovered.

With near-total air supremacy, US forces launched strikes against the Japanese fleet from extreme range. The 51 Helldivers committed suffered 46 lost, of which 32 were due to running out of fuel. The 26 Dauntlesses suffered one shot down and one crashed on landing. Even discounting the losses due to miscalculations about range, the Helldiver was greatly outperformed by an aircraft it was intended to replace.

The SB2C-4 went into production with all the improvements that had trickled through SB2C-3 production and incorporated the ability to launch rockets from under-wing mountings. SB2C-5 was essentially the same

aircraft albeit with increased fuel tankage, and the SC2C-6 variant – with a more powerful engine – was successfully tested but arrived too late for war service. By this stage in the conflict, needs were changing. Level bombers were preferred to dive-bombers, and fighter bombers could offer support to troops ashore at least as effectively using rockets.

The Helldiver was withdrawn from carrier service in 1947, though it remained in reserve until 1950. The last Helldivers remaining in service were with Italy. They were retired in 1959.

A Curtiss SB2C-5 Helldiver from Bombing Squadron Ten (VB-10), USS *Intrepid* (CV-11), flies over Tientsin, China, as the city is reoccupied by the Allies, 5 September 1945.

Douglas TBD Devastator

The Devastator was considered an advanced aircraft when it entered service in 1937. However, by the time it saw action, it was already obsolescent.

The Devastator achieved a number of firsts for the US carrier forces – the first carrier-based aircraft with an all-glazed cockpit canopy, the first all-metal aircraft, the first mass-produced monoplane and the first aircraft to have hydraulically folding wings. The initial purchase of 110 was the largest peacetime order made by the US Navy up to that point.

Additional aircraft, ordered to replace some lost in training accidents, brought production up to 129. Although designated a torpedo bomber, the TBD was intended to carry out conventional bombing as well.

To this end, it was fitted with a Norden bombsight protected by clamshell doors when not in use. To use the sight, the aimer had to lie prone beneath the pilot's position. Bomb load was 454kg (1000lb) or one torpedo. Its armament of two 7.62mm (0.3in) machine guns, one fixed forward and one in a flexible mount at the rear of the cockpit, was considered adequate for a strike platform at the time.

Trials were highly successful, with only minor modifications required. In October 1937, VT-3, serving aboard USS *Saratoga*, took delivery of the first examples. By the end of the year, all carriers had received the Devastator. However, by the outbreak of war, the TBD was due for replacement. The Grumman TBF was selected but had not yet been delivered.

Battle of the Coral Sea

The Devastator made an impressive debut, sinking the Japanese carriers Shokaku and – along with SBDs – Shoho at the Battle of the Coral Sea in May 1942. A month later, at the Battle of Midway, heavy losses were taken without effect upon the enemy. This was largely due to the unreliable Mk XIII torpedo, a problem

Douglas TBD-1

Weight: (Maximum take-off) 4624kg (10,194lb)
Dimensions: Length: 10.67m (35ft), Wingspan: 15.24m (50ft), Height: 4.6m (15ft 1in)
Powerplant: One 670kW (900hp) Pratt & Whitney R-1830-64 Twin Wasp 14-cylinder air-cooled radial piston engine
Speed: 332km/h (206mph)
Range: 1152km (715 miles)
Ceiling: 5900m (19,500ft)
Crew: 3
Armament: One 7.62mm (0.30in) M1919 machine gun fixed forward-firing in cowling, one 7.62mm (0.30in) M1919 machine gun flexibly mounted in rear cockpit; up to 453kg (1000lb) bomb load or one 907kg (2000lb) Mk XIII torpedo

Douglas TBD-1 Devastator

Pictured in pre-war US Navy markings, this TBD-1 served with VT-6 and wears the squadron's white albatross insignia under the windscreen.

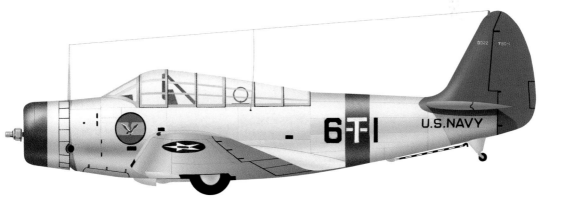

that dogged the US Navy during the early war. Although it was overall a good aircraft – reliable, easy to fly and well suited to carrier landings – the Devastator was vulnerable to enemy fighters and anti-aircraft fire. As a result, the surviving examples were relegated to less dangerous roles, mostly as trainers. The Devastator was completely out of service by December 1944.

A variant, designated TBD-1A, was developed in response to Dutch interest in a coastal patrol aircraft. This was to be a floatplane, and it might have given useful service.

However, the overrun of the Netherlands by Axis forces ensured this project never developed beyond the prototype. This saw out its days as a development platform for improved torpedoes, where its low minimum speed and overall stability proved to be an asset. The TBD-1A was retired in 1943.

Douglas AD-1 Skyraider

Arriving just too late to contribute to World War II, but representing lessons hard learned during it, the Skyraider played an important part in subsequent conflicts in Korea and Vietnam.

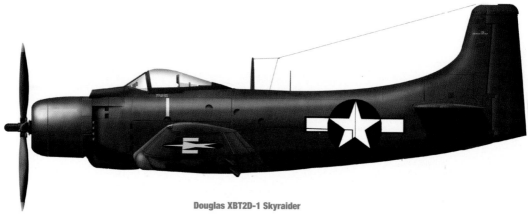

Douglas XBT2D-1 Skyraider
Designer Ed Heinemann worked out that for every 45kg (100lb) of weight lost, combat radius increased by 35km (22 miles). A rigorous weight reduction programme transformed the basic XBT2D-1 design into the prototype of the superlative Skyraider, shown here.

No matter how many aircraft could be carried aboard a vessel, operations were limited by the types available. The solution was to create a single design capable of both torpedo and bombing attacks.

Douglass first offered the XSB2D-1: a two-seat model with two 20mm (0.79in) cannon in the wings and two remote-controlled turrets, each mounting twin 12.7mm (0.5in) machine guns. The XSB2D-1 carried 1900kg (4200lb) of ordnance, but it was heavy and difficult to maintain.

The US Navy requested a single-seat version, with the turrets removed and additional fuel. It was designated the BTD-1 Destroyer and had the advantage, over the two-seat original, that it could carry two torpedoes.

The BTD-1 was not a success. It was simply too heavy, and production was cancelled after 28 were built.

Douglas AD-1 Skyraider

Weight: (Maximum take-off) 8178kg (18,029lb)

Dimensions: Length: 12m (39ft 3in), Wingspan: 15.24m (50ft), Height: 4.8m (17ft 8in)

Powerplant: One 1865kW (2500hp) Wright R-3350-24W Duplex Cyclone 18-cylinder air-cooled radial piston engine

Speed: 517km/h (321mph)

Range: 2500km (1553 miles)

Ceiling: 7925m (26,000ft)

Crew: 1

Armament: Two (later four) 20mm (0.78in) AN/M3 cannon fixed forward-firing in wings; bomb load up to 3629kg (8000lb)

Douglas then redeveloped it, removing all excess weight and simplifying the aircraft as much as possible. This new version first flew in March 1945 and went into production as the AD-1 Skyraider.

Korean War service

During the Korean conflict of 1950–53, the Skyraider proved its worth as a strike and support platform, remaining in production until 1947 despite the availability of jet aircraft. The last examples in service were in the early 1980s with Gabon.

Preparing for take-off

A Douglas AD-1 Skyraider, fully loaded with bombs, takes off from the deck of an aircraft carrier for an attack on enemy targets in Korea, 1952.

Consolidated TBY Sea Wolf

Deemed superior to the Avenger, the strange-looking TBY Sea Wolf was ordered in large numbers but was doomed to obscurity by delays and bad luck and never saw combat service.

The Sea Wolf was designed by Vought to fulfill the same 1939 specification as the Grumman TBF Avenger and flew for the first time as the XBTU-1 on 22 December 1941. Flight testing during early 1942 revealed the Sea Wolf possessed greater speed and superior range to the Avenger, and an order for 1100 TBYs was placed by the US Navy.

Vought was at full capacity producing the F4U Corsair and unable to meet such an order, so production was contracted to Consolidated-Vultee as the TBY-1. A converted truck factory in Pennsylvania was to be used to build the Sea Wolves, but delays ensued as both the conversion process and workforce training took several months.

Trial and mishap

Meanwhile further time was lost when the entire tail unit of the aircraft was ripped off during arrested landing trials, necessitating lengthy repairs. Unfortunately the newly repaired tail unit was then badly damaged in a collision with the propeller of an out

of control training aircraft resulting in further repair work.

Vought engineers used the enforced delays to redesign and improve both the undercarriage and bomb bay doors and fit an improved model of R-2800 engine. ASV radar was added as standard in a pod on the starboard wing and in this form the Sea Wolf became the TBY-2.

Production

Deliveries of production aircraft only began during November 1944, by which time the TBF Avengers equipped every torpedo bomber unit in the Navy and it was clear that the Sea Wolf, despite its superior performance, would not be required for operational service.

Limited production continued throughout 1945 resulting in the delivery of 180 TBY-2s, which were used as training aircraft. Order numbers were progressively reduced until the entire programme was cancelled in August 1945.

Consolidated TBY-2

Weight (maximum take-off): 8951kg (18,940lbs)

Dimensions: Length: 11.94m (39ft 2in), Wingspan: 17.53m (56ft 11in), Height: 4.72m (15ft 6in)

Powerplant: One 1600kW (2100hp) Pratt & Whitney R-2800-22 Double Wasp 18-cylinder air-cooled radial piston engine

Speed: 502km/h (312mph)

Range: 1650km (1025 miles)

Ceiling: 9000m (29,400ft)

Crew: 3

Armament: One 12.7mm (0.5in) M2 Browning machine gun fixed forward-firing in cowling, two 12.7mm (0.5in) M2 Browning machine guns fixed forward-firing in wings, one 12.7mm (0.5in) M2 Browning machine gun in rear turret, one 7.62mm (0.3in) M1919 Browning machine gun flexibly mounted in ventral position; up to 907kg (2000lbs) bomb load or one 907kg (2000lb) Mark XIII torpedo or Mark 24 acoustic homing torpedo in bomb bay

Consolidated TBY-2 Sea Wolf

A US Navy Consolidated TBY-2 Sea Wolf (BuNo 31463) sitting on the flight line. Note the APS-4 radar, zero-length rocket launchers and the machine gun pods under the wings.

Martin AM-1 Mauler

The Mauler represented a shift away from the concept of separate torpedo and bomber aircraft, creating a multi-role strike platform that arrived too late to take part in World War II.

In 1943, the US Navy requested prototypes for a single-strike aircraft that could carry out both torpedo and bombing attacks. The Curtiss XBTC was one of those selected for development, along with what became the Mauler. The requirement specified that the new strike platform would use the Pratt & Whitney R-4360 Wasp Major engine and that the airframe be non-experimental.

Structural issues

Despite not taking risks with the airframe, serious problems were encountered during development. Aerodynamic issues emerged from the first flight, made in August 1944, and there were serious structural problems with the rear fuselage.

In addition to a tendency to bounce on landing, which could cause a failure to engage the arrestor wire, one aircraft tore itself in half when it did successfully engage. Trials concluded that the Mauler was particularly difficult to operate during

Martin AM-1 Mauler

An impressive aircraft, the Mauler was intended to be a relatively simple 'low-risk' option for a single-seat attack aircraft, but was itself sidelined by an even simpler aircraft in the form of the Skyraider. This reserve AM-1 was based at Glenview Naval Air Station in the early 1950s.

long-distance or instrument flights. Nevertheless, an order for 750 was placed in January 1945.

'Awful Monster'

Despite being described as an 'Awful Monster' in some quarters, the AM-1 Mauler set an unofficial record of 4830kg (10,648lb), the greatest load carried by a single-seat piston-engine aircraft. Its armament of four 20mm (0.79in) cannon and up to 4830kg (10,648lb) was certainly impressive, but its inferior performance compared to aircraft such as the Skyraider ensured that its service life was over by 1953.

Martin AM-1 Mauler

Weight: (Maximum take-off) 11,700kg (25,794lb)
Dimensions: Length: 12.57m (41ft 3in), Wingspan: 15.24m (50ft), Height: 5.13m (16ft 10in)
Powerplant: One 2200kW (3000hp) Pratt & Whitney R-4360 Wasp Major 28-cylinder air-cooled radial piston engine
Speed: 538km/h (334mph)
Range: 2452km (1524 miles)
Ceiling: 8200m (27,000ft)
Crew: 1
Armament: Four 20mm (0.79in) T-31 cannon fixed forward-firing in wings; up to 4830kg (10,648lb) bomb load on 15 external hardpoints

TRANSPORTS & FLYING BOATS

The development of the modern transport aircraft ran in parallel to that of the strategic bomber in the US, the hugely successful Douglas DC-3/C-47 in particular influenced the design of long-range combat aircraft just as it was revolutionizing aerial transport worldwide. Flying boats were primarily useful for scouting and rescue, but did at times attempt attacks on enemy ships.

The following aircraft are featured in this chapter:

- Douglas C-47 Skytrain
- Curtiss C-46 Commando
- Martin PBM Mariner
- Grumman J2F-4 Duck
- Consolidated PBY Catlina
- Vought OS2U Kingfisher
- Curtiss SO3C-1 Seamew

The American transport plane Douglas C-47 'Skytrain' (military version of the DC-3 Dakota) flying over the pyramids of Giza in Egypt. 1944.

Douglas C-47 Skytrain

Over 16,000 DC-3s and C-47s were constructed. Despite dating from the 1930s, nearly 200 are still in service today.

First flying in 1935, the Douglas DC-3 was over-engineered from the start. This created a very rugged aircraft, the good safety record of which was a factor in its success as a commercial airliner. The civilian DC-3 could carry 2725kg (6000lb) of cargo or either 21 or 28 passengers.

Its cabin was unpressurized, limiting maximum altitude but also increasing the longevity of the airframe due to reduced stresses. Its success was phenomenal; almost 85 per cent of airliners operating in the USA in the early 1940s were DC-3a.

Cargolifter and staff transporter

In 1936, the USAAF evaluated the Douglas DC-2 for military use. This was the predecessor of the DC-3, a twin-engine design capable of transporting 12 passengers. The aircraft purchased were designated C-33 in cargolifter configuration and C-34 when set up as staff transports. They were followed by a prototype designated C-38, created by matching the DC-3 tail assembly to a DC-2 fuselage. The production version, of which 35 were built, was designated

Douglas C-47A Skytrain

This USAAF C-47A (42-100444), based at Hailakandi, India, was used as a glider tug during the Burma campaign. The aircraft crashed at Warazup, Burma, on 19 April 1945.

C-39. A developed version of the DC-3 was ordered in 1941 as the mainstay of USAAF transportation services. Designated C-47 Skytrain, it featured modifications to the cargo door and a hook for glider towing but was otherwise nearly identical to the civilian DC-3.

The decision to create a major airlift capability was one of the most strategically vital initiatives of the World War II era and represented bold forward thinking. In the modern era, large-scale transportation and logistics movement by air is a well-proven concept, but at the time, the idea was new and perhaps controversial.

Versatile workhorse

The C-47 retained the same cargo capacity as the DC-3, though its doors were larger and could admit a small artillery weapon or jeep without

Douglas C-47A

Weight (maximum take-off): 11,794kg (25,947lb)
Dimensions: Length: 19.43m (63ft 9in), Wingspan: 29.11m (95ft 6in), Height: 5.18m (17ft)
Powerplant: Two 895kW (1200hp) Pratt & Whitney R-1830-92 Twin Wasp radial engines
Maximum Speed: 365km/h (226mph)
Range: 2414km (1597 miles)
Ceiling: 7070m (24,000ft)
Crew: 4
Armament: N/A

dismantling. It could carry up to 28 fully equipped personnel and deliver paratroops or tow gliders into an assault. This was never a comfortable experience, however, with the C-47 earning the epithet 'vomit comet' in some quarters.

In addition to the USAAF, the C-47 was operated by the US Navy, which designated it R4D, as well as British and Australian forces, which nicknamed it the Dakota. The Canadian version was known as the C-120. It was widely referred to as the Gooney Bird. There is some doubt as to whether the C-47 was given this name or inherited it from the R2D, a variant of the preceding DC-2, which was the first aircraft to land on Midway Island.

Whatever names it was called, the C-47 was invaluable to the war effort.

Indeed, General Dwight Eisenhower listed it among the four 'tools of victory' – the others being the Jeep, the bazooka and the atomic bomb. It is notable that two of the four were utility and transportation equipment rather than weapons.

Seven standard variants of the C-47 were constructed, with some other conversions when necessary, but by far, the greatest contribution it made to the war was in the field of logistics. The tough C-47 could operate from short and rather poor airstrips, enabling it to fly supplies into areas otherwise only reachable by airdrop.

Over the Hump

Allied forces fighting in China and Burma benefited particularly from C-47 support. Supplies and

reinforcements were flown in from India, and casualties extracted the same way. This required a long flight over the Himalayas, and this rather significant obstacle became known as 'the Hump'. Airborne logistics kept the Allied troops in the region in fighting condition, but gradually they were driven back.

The turning point was the Battle of Imphal and Kohima, sometimes known as the 'Stalingrad of the East'. In some of the most desperate close-quarters fighting of the war, the Allies managed to halt the Japanese advance despite being surrounded at Kohima.

Some 12,000 troops were flown in and 13,000 casualties evacuated, with 19,000 tons of supplies either landed or dropped from low altitude. Kept supplied, the Allies were able – barely – to hold out, while the Japanese, who had relied on capturing supplies from

C-47 transport planes are loaded with paratroopers at Jackson Drome near Port Moresby, New Guinea, just prior to take-off on an aerial assault at the Markham River area. In a group to the left, General Douglas MacArthur and Lieutenant General George Keaney, US Army, Commanding General, Fifth Air Force, confer during this first use of parachute troops in the South West Pacific Area, September 1943.

a retreating enemy, suffered dreadful privations and eventually had to retreat.

The success of operations such as these depended not only on the possession of a suitable transport aircraft but also on an effective system for using it. C-47s assigned to a supply mission were grouped into 'serials' of up to 50 aircraft, each assigned a temporary number, and were loaded according to a detailed plan intended to minimize unloading time at the far end.

Paratroop and glider operations

Standard C-47s and a specialist paratroop version designated C-53 Skytrooper were used to deliver airborne forces either by paradrop or towed glider. Paratroops and glider forces landed ahead of the Allied invasion of Sicily in July 1943 and were tasked with seizing strategic objectives inland ahead of the D-Day landings in June 1944. C-47s dropped over 50,000 troops in the initial days of the landings. When dropping paratroops, it was standard practice

to build larger formations out of a 'V' of three aircraft, with three Vs of three creating a V of 9. Subsequent Vs of 9 would pass over the target area in rapid succession, in theory ensuring a tight drop. In practice, however, some scattering was inevitable. C-47s towing gliders operated in pairs with the second aircraft to the right of and behind the leader.

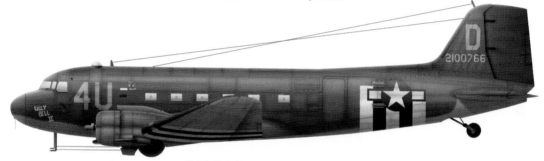

C-47A Skytrain

C-47A-70-DL (serial number 42-100766), named 'Lilly Bell II', from the 89th Troop Carrier Squadron, 438th Troop Carrier Group, based at Greenham Common, Berkshire, England, October 1944. 'Lilly Bell II' was sadly lost in an accident after its cargo shifted mid-flight on 25 October 1944.

C-47A Skytrain

C-47A-65-DL, named 'Buzz Buggy', from the 81st Troop Carrier Squadron, 436th Troop Carrier Group, based at Membury, Berkshire, England, Winter 1944. Painted in the trademark invasion stripes, 'Buzz Buggy' participated in the airborne assaults on Normandy, Holland and Germany in 1944–45.

Douglas C-47A

Weight (maximum take-off): 11,794kg (25,947lb)
Dimensions: Length: 19.43m (63ft 9in), Wingspan: 29.11m (95ft 6in), Height: 5.18m (17ft)
Powerplant: Two 895kW (1200hp) Pratt & Whitney R-1830-92 Twin Wasp radial engines
Maximum Speed: 365km/h (226mph)
Range: 2414km (1597 miles)
Ceiling: 7070m (24,000ft)
Crew: 4 (pilot, co-pilot, navigator, radio operator); 27 troops
Armament: N/A

Some 1438 C-47s, most of them operated by US personnel, took part in Operation Market Garden, an audacious attempt to shorten the war by seizing the Rhine bridges around Arnhem – 34,600 airborne troops preceded the ground advance; 20,011 landed by glider and 14,589 by parachute. Additional equipment and supplies were airdropped, but

ultimately, the lightly equipped airborne troops were overrun before the main assault reached its target.

Parachute forces made a smaller but extremely difficult assault from C-47s against the island of Corregidor in February 1945. The only suitable – if that word can be used – point to land at was a hill named Topside, necessitating a tightly coordinated

Douglas C-47-DL

Weight (maximum take-off): 11,794kg (25,947lb)
Dimensions: Length: 19.43m (63ft 9in), Wingspan: 29.11m (95ft 6in), Height: 5.18m (17ft)
Powerplant: Two 895kW (1200hp) Pratt & Whitney R-1830-92 Twin Wasp radial engines
Maximum Speed: 365km/h (226mph)
Range: 2414km (1597 miles)
Ceiling: 7070m (24,000ft)
Crew: 4 (pilot, co-pilot, navigator, radio operator); 27 troops
Armament: N/A

C-47-DL Skytrain

C-47-DL (serial number 41-38601), named 'Swamp Rat', from the 6th Troop Carrier Squadron, 374th Troop Carrier Group, based at Dobodura Airfield, New Guinea, November 1942. 'Swamp Rat' was shot down by Japanese A6M Zero fighters on 26 November 1942, near the north coast of New Guinea.

jump from low altitude. C-47s of 317th Troop Carrier Group succeeded in delivering most of their paratroopers onto the hill, resulting in fierce fighting. After several days, the island was taken by a combination of airborne forces and a beach assault.

Other service

C-47s served in a great many roles, including air defence evaluation, medical evacuation and staff transport. A chain of C-47s flew back and forth across the Pacific from island runways ferrying personnel home and bringing replacements out. Other aircraft were modified for high-altitude work or operations in arctic conditions.

Service continued after the war, notably in the Berlin Airlift of 1948–49. As tensions increased between the Soviet Union and its former allies, the Western-controlled part of Berlin was blockaded. Rather than give in to Soviet demands, a massive airlift of food and fuel kept the city supplied. C-47s were instrumental in delivering the enormous amount of supplies required to feed Berlin's civilian population.

Some examples left US service in the post-war years, going to other nations or private operators, but the C-47 remained an important part of the US inventory in the Korean conflict. By the time of the Vietnam War, electronic warfare variants were available, carrying the designation EC-47 followed by an N, P or Q to indicate the engines fitted. The C-47 also provided the airframe for a close support platform.

Designated AC-47 and known as 'Puff the Magic Dragon' or 'Spooky', the C-47 gunship mounted three 7.62mm (0.3in) miniguns to fire from its left side. Rather than strafing a target by flying over it, or making a head-on attack with bombs or rockets, the AC-47 was intended to circle the target at relatively low speed. The great endurance of the aircraft permitted it to remain on-station for long periods, providing support as requested or when targets presented themselves. The airborne gunship proved a great success and is credited with turning the tide of many engagements. The AC-47 was replaced in this role by the AC-130. Based on the Hercules, the AC-130 carries heavier weapons but fulfils the same function.

Post-military usage

As the C-47 was replaced in service by more modern aircraft, many examples went to other forces or civilian operators. Some examples are still flying, typically in remote areas where the infrastructure to support more advanced aircraft is not available. The numbers dwindle over time, of course, either due to maintenance problems or the occasional crash – but on the other hand, now and then a DC-3/C-47 is rebuilt and returned to flying service.

Some surviving examples are given a new lease of life by conversion to turboprop propulsion by Basler Turbo Conversions. The conversion process involves lengthening the fuselage and a complete rebuild, to the point where the resulting BT-67 is considered a new and different aircraft for legal purposes. In addition to civilian operators, the BT-67 is used as a transport by some national militaries and in a gunship role, similar to the AC-47, by the Colombian Air Force.

American paratroopers ready to embark in their Douglas C-47 Skytrain transport aircraft, as part of the wider assault on German-occupied Sicily, 10 July 1943. In total, 144 C-47 Skytrain transports took part in the operation.

Douglas C-47 Skytrain

The original military version of the DC-3 had four crew (pilot, co-pilot, navigator, and radio operator) and seats for 27 troops. Models fitted for casualty evacuation could carry 18 stretcher cases and a medical crew of three.

Douglas C-47 Skytrain

Weight (maximum take-off): 11,794kg (25,947lb)
Dimensions: Length: 19.43m (63ft 9in), Wingspan: 29.11m (95ft 6in), Height: 5.18m (17ft)
Powerplant: Two 895kW (1200hp) Pratt & Whitney R-1830-92 Twin Wasp radial engines
Maximum Speed: 365km/h (226mph)
Range: 2414km (1597 miles)
Ceiling: 7070m (24,000ft)
Crew: 4; 27 troops or 18 stretcher cases
Armament: N/A

Curtiss C-46 Commando

The C-46 Commando served almost exclusively in the Pacific theatre, not reaching Europe until the very last weeks of World War II.

The aircraft that became the C-46 Commando was initially developed as a pressurized-cabin airliner, intended to be a larger competitor to the Douglas DC-3. Work began in 1936, with first flight in 1940 under the designation CW-20T. This twin-rudder design was unsatisfactory and was redeveloped as CW-20A with a more conventional tail assembly.

New order

At this time, the USAAF was in need of large numbers of transport aircraft and placed an order for 200 slightly modified CW-20Bs, which entered service under the designation C-46. After the first 25 aircraft, later production was to C-46A standard, with a cargo floor and simplifications to the fuselage. A total of 1479 C-46 and C-46As were constructed, most of which served with the USAAF, though some were provided to the Marine Corps and later the Navy.

War service

The C-46A was the largest twin-engine aircraft used by the USAAF. It could carry 40–45 troops in combat gear, or a total of 4550kg (10,000lb) of cargo. Its primary contribution to the war was transporting equipment and supplies over 'the Hump' (the Himalayas) from India to China.

Losses were significant, though not always due to enemy action. The C-46 was operating in a harsh environment, making high-altitude crossings of the Himalayas and using very basic facilities. In addition, it was subject to fuel and hydraulic leaks.

Korea and Vietnam

Having worked out most of its problems, the C-46 was returned to service for the Korean conflict, delivering both cargo and paratroopers and later serving in the Vietnam War.

Curtiss C-46F Commando

Twin-engined cargo transport aircraft, equipped with single cargo doors on both sides of the fuselage, fitted with square cut wingtips. In total, 234 C-46Fs were built.

Curtiss C-46F

Weight (maximum take-off): 20,412kg (45,000lb)

Dimensions: Length: 23.27m (76ft 4in), Wingspan: 32.92m (108ft), Height: 6.63m (21ft 9in)

Powerplant: Two 1500kW (2000hp) Pratt & Whitney R-2800-51 Double Wasp 18-cylinder air-cooled radial piston engines

Maximum Speed: 430km/h (270mph)

Range: 5070 km (3150 mi)

Ceiling: 7500m (24,500ft)

Crew: 4 or 5; 40 troops or 30 stretcher patients, or 4550kg (10,000lb) cargo

Armament: N/A

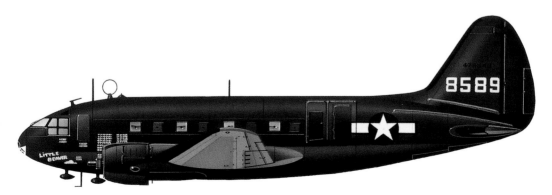

Martin PBM Mariner

In the early 1930s, the Martin Aircraft Company turned away from the maritime patrol market in favour of the flying boat airliner field.

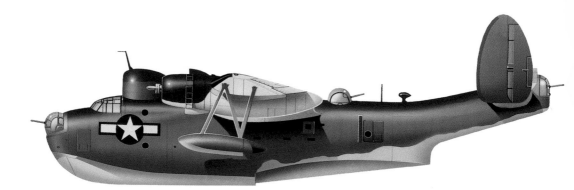

Unable to compete with Boeing, the company returned to designing naval aircraft and produced a four-engine design named Model 160. This was revised into the twin-engine Model 162 and demonstrated as a ¼ scale mock-up. Despite a requirement for a full-sized prototype, the US Navy ordered this aircraft as XPBM-1 – Patrol Bomber, Martin.

Atlantic patrols

The XPBM-1 first flew in February 1939, with deliveries commencing in September 1940. Its initial deployment was with VP-55 and VP-56, patrolling the western Atlantic. An additional 379 examples were ordered just before the USA joined the war. These were PBM-3s, with powered weapon turrets and improved Wright R-2600-12 engines. The name 'Mariner' was not assigned at this time; it came from the British – two took delivery of some PBMs but decided to use their own Short Sunderland instead.

Like other flying boats, the XPBM-1 needed to keep its engines high above

Martin PBM-3 Mariner

This aircraft is painted in a Pacific War colour scheme. The large search radar is apparent above and behind the main cockpit, enclosed in a streamlined fairing.

saltwater spray as it would damage them. To this end, it used a high gull wing and retractable balance floats, which were replaced with fixed floats on later models. The internal bomb bay could hold a 1814kg (4000lb) load, which could include torpedoes on some variants. Defensive armament initially consisted of a single 12.7mm (0.5in) machine gun in the nose and dorsal turrets plus others in waist and tail positions. The turret guns were increased to dual-mount weapons in later versions.

U-Boat hunters

Flying boats were an important weapon in the battle to protect shipping from submarine attack, but this was no one-sided conflict. U-boats were not defenceless against aircraft by the middle of the war,

---

Martin PBM-3 Mariner

Weight (maximum take-off): 26,253kg (57,878lb)

Dimensions: Length: 24.38m (80ft), Wingspan: 35.97m (118ft), Height: 8.23m (27ft)

Powerplant: Two 1194kW (1600hp) Wright R-2600-6 14-cylinder radial engines

Maximum Speed: 338km/h (210mph)

Range: 3597km (2235 miles)

Ceiling: 6095m (20,000ft)

Crew: 7–8

Armament: Eight 12.7mm (.50 cal) machine guns in nose, dorsal turrets, waist and tail; plus up to 746kg (1646lbs) of bombs, torpedoes and depth charges

---

having been provided with anti-aircraft weapons, including quad-mounted 20mm (0.79in) automatic cannon. A U-boat commander sighting an approaching aircraft had a critical choice to make: either crash-dive and hope to slip away or remain on the surface and fight. A misjudged dive would leave the boat with its stern out of the water as the aircraft made its attack run. Several Mariners were lost to U-boats whose captains decided or were forced to stay on the surface. Nevertheless, Mariners sank 10 U-boats during the course of the war, out of a total of 29 destroyed by patrol aircraft.

Specialist versions

Various specialist versions were created, notably the PBM-3S long-range variant. Greater endurance was achieved by removing as much weight as possible, while the PBM-3R had its armour and defensive armament removed to create a transport aircraft. The last model to enter service, in 1944, was the PBM-5. It represented an all-round upgrade with better engines, radar and communications equipment. It was also capable of using Jet Assisted Take-off (JATO) units to shorten its takeoff distance. After the war, an amphibious variant emerged that used a retractable undercarriage. These engaged in post-war activities such as polar exploration and support of the atomic bomb test programme. Some Mariners took part in the Korean conflict, flying coastal night patrols.

Martin PBM-3 Mariner
A US Navy Martin PBM-3 Mariner of Patrol Squadron 74 (74-P-3), 1942. The same aircraft is shown in the picture above.

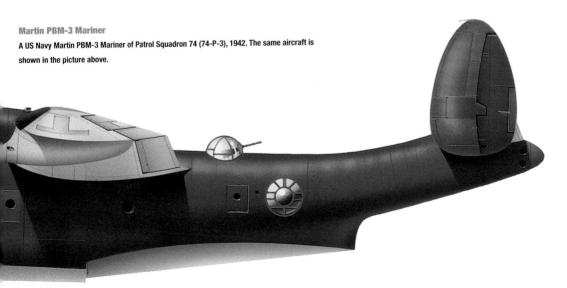

Grumman J2F-4 Duck

The Grumman J2F Duck was developed from the outset as a communications and utility platform. It served as a transport, reconnaissance and anti-submarine aircraft.

The J2F was originally developed as the JF-1 with a Twin Wasp engine. It first flew in April 1933 and was adopted by the Argentine Navy as well as the US Navy and Coast Guard. 48 of this version were built before it was improved by replacing its Twin Wasp engine with a Wright Cyclone.

The upgraded version, designated J2F, had few other differences from the original. No weapons were fitted as standard, but a cabin space between the pilot and navigator could be used for various purposes.

It was designed to carry two seated passengers or a casualty on a stretcher. The aircraft also housed photographic equipment when a Duck was deployed in the photographic reconnaissance role.

Duck of all trades

Some Ducks were outfitted with bomb racks and defensive machine

Grumman J2F-3 Duck

Flown for Rear Admiral Brown, Supt., this J2F-3 (1569) was stationed at the Naval Academy in Annapolis, Maryland.

guns for patrol work in the Caribbean, while around 20 were assigned as transports for high-ranking officers and other VIPs. Later models were given target-towing equipment, some of which were operated by the USAAF.

The final variant was designated J2F-6 and was built by Colombia aircraft instead of Grumman. This version was able to undertake limited anti-submarine work.

Ultimately, 584 Ducks were built, and like many utility platforms, it remained in service long after World War II. The last operator, Peru, retired its Ducks in 1964.

Grumman J2F-3

Weight: (Maximum take-off) 3493kg (7700lb)

Dimensions: Length: 10.36m (34ft), Wingspan: 11.89m (39ft), Height: 4.24m (13ft 11in)

Powerplant: One 670kW (900hp) Wright R-1820-54 Cyclone 9-cylinder, air-cooled, radial piston engine

Speed: 310km/h (190mph)

Range: 1260km (780 miles)

Ceiling: 6100m (20,000ft)

Crew: 2

Armament: One 7.62mm (0.3in) Browning M1919 machine gun flexibly mounted in rear cockpit; up to 295kg (650lb) bomb load

Consolidated PBY Catalina

The Consolidated Catalina was used mainly for transportation, long-range patrols and rescue missions, as well as anti-submarine work. It contributed to both the Atlantic and Pacific campaigns.

Beginning in 1928, Consolidated developed a maritime patrol aircraft designated XPY-1 and unofficially named 'Admiral', hoping for sales to the US Navy. Ultimately, the naval contract went to the Martin combat but the aircraft, now known as the Commodore, gained a good reputation as an airliner.

XP2Y-1 Ranger

Consolidated's next offering, the XP2Y-1 Ranger, first flew in 1932. Initially, it had three engines, with one located above the parasol main wing. However, it went into production as a twin-engined model. The Ranger was a sesquiplane, with a smaller second

wing supporting its stabilizing floats. An order for the first Rangers was placed in July 1931, with improved versions appearing over time. However, as early as 1933, the US Navy saw the need for an improved maritime patrol aircraft. Initial design work began in response to a US Navy request to a 1933, and in due course, Consolidated put forward the XP3Y-1, which bore a resemblance to the Ranger but was a great improvement overall. The XP3Y-1 did away with the lower wing. Its single large parasol wing was internally braced, making external struts unnecessary, and the balancing floats were designed to retract to the wingtips in flight.

A Consolidated PBY-5A Catalina patrol bomber in flight during 1942.

The ungainly framework between wing and fuselage was encased in a pylon, creating a more elegant and aerodynamic profile.

PBY designation

Trials indicated the XP3Y-1 to be significantly superior to earlier flying boat designs. Its capability to carry a 908kg (2000lb) bomb load resulted in redesignation to Patrol Bomber (PB), with the Y indicating a Consolidated design. The name Catalina was originally used by the RAF but eventually adopted by the US as well.

Early service

The initial order for 60 aircraft, placed in June 1935, specified relatively little change from the original design other than some modifications to the tail section and improved engines. The first deliveries were to VP-11F in October 1936, with a total of 16 US squadrons receiving Catalinas by the end of 1941. Other users included Britain, Russia, Australia, Canada and New Zealand.

Between 1936 and 1939, new models appeared. The PBY-2, PBY-3 and PBY-4 incorporated only minor changes and gained improved engines

each time. The PBY-5 emerged in September 1940, joining the forces assigned to the Neutrality Patrol. This measure assisted Britain far more than the Axis powers, with a great many German vessels intercepted after their positions were reported. The mission gradually expanded, with US naval forces escorting convoys headed for Britain and ordered to attack vessels threatening them.

Wartime service

At the end of the 1930s, the PBY was thought to be becoming obsolete,

A Consolidated PBY-5A patrol bomber drops a Mark XIII torpedo during tests in 1943.

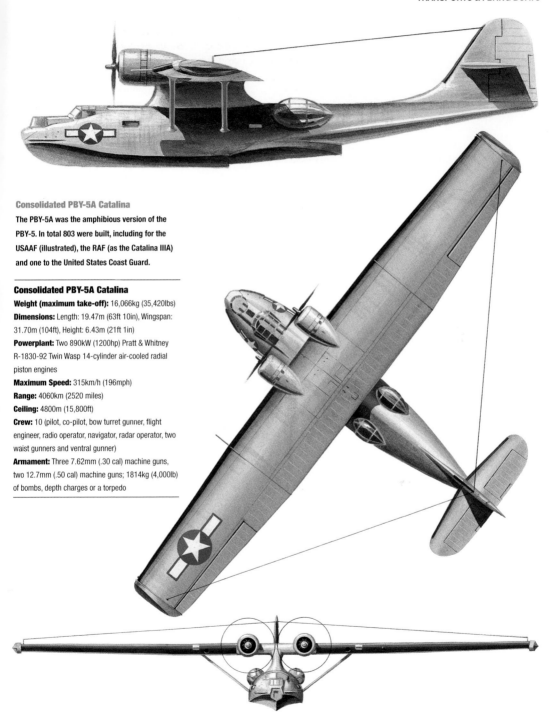

Consolidated PBY-5A Catalina

The PBY-5A was the amphibious version of the PBY-5. In total 803 were built, including for the USAAF (illustrated), the RAF (as the Catalina IIIA) and one to the United States Coast Guard.

Consolidated PBY-5A Catalina

Weight (maximum take-off): 16,066kg (35,420lbs)

Dimensions: Length: 19.47m (63ft 10in), Wingspan: 31.70m (104ft), Height: 6.43m (21ft 1in)

Powerplant: Two 890kW (1200hp) Pratt & Whitney R-1830-92 Twin Wasp 14-cylinder air-cooled radial piston engines

Maximum Speed: 315km/h (196mph)

Range: 4060km (2520 miles)

Ceiling: 4800m (15,800ft)

Crew: 10 (pilot, co-pilot, bow turret gunner, flight engineer, radio operator, navigator, radar operator, two waist gunners and ventral gunner)

Armament: Three 7.62mm (.30 cal) machine guns, two 12.7mm (.50 cal) machine guns; 1814kg (4,000lb) of bombs, depth charges or a torpedo

Consolidated OA-10 Catalina

The Americans used a large number of Catalinas in the search-and-rescue role, especially in the Pacific theatre, designated OA-10.

Consolidated OA-10

Weight (maximum take-off): 16,066kg (35,420lbs)
Dimensions: Length: 19.47m (63ft 10in), Wingspan: 31.70m (104ft), Height: 6.15m (20ft 2in)
Powerplant: Two 895kW (1200hp) Pratt & Whitney R1830-92 Twin Wasp radial piston engines
Maximum Speed: 288km/h (175mph)
Range: 4900km (3045 miles)
Ceiling: 4480m (18,100ft)
Crew: 7–9
Armament: N/A

unable to be upgraded any further. However, with war looming, there was no time to develop a new aircraft. Production expanded to meet a sudden need to patrol vast areas of ocean, beginning with an order for 200 PBY-5s, which featured improved engines. It was followed by the PBY-6, which gained a taller tail and better defensive armament in addition to a new radar system. Other companies built almost identical aircraft under local designations.

Catalinas based at Pearl Harbor attacked one of the Japanese submarines involved in the raid but suffered heavy losses on the ground. However, PBYs of VP-44 provided reconnaissance data that proved instrumental to successful strikes on the Japanese fleet at the Battle of Midway. Radar-equipped Catalinas attacked Japanese shipping at night off Guadalcanal and ground targets in the Aleutian Islands.

True flying boat

Most PBYs were true flying boats, which could only be brought onto land using specialist beaching gear. The PBY-5A variant, first flying in

November 1939, had a retractable undercarriage for amphibious operations. It was adopted under the designation OA-10 by the USAAF for its Emergency Rescue Squadrons. Catalinas had undertaken rescue operations throughout their career, but from 1943, they served as an enabler for long-range bombing missions against the Japanese Home Islands, rescuing crews of damaged or out-of-fuel B-29 Superfortresses.

The Atlantic war

In the Atlantic, the most famous exploit of a PBY was locating the German surface raiders *Bismarck* and *Prince Eugen*, allowing a powerful force of surface ships to make an intercept. Most of the time, contributions were more low-key.

Catalinas did engage and, in some cases, sink U-boats, but their presence had a more subtle effect on the Battle of the Atlantic. By making it too hazardous to surface during the day, patrol aircraft limited the ability of U-boats to recharge their batteries and thus degraded their efficiency. Catalinas also occasionally engaged enemy patrol aircraft.

Consolidated PBY Catalina Mk.IIA
Weight (maximum take-off): 16,066kg (35,420lbs)
Dimensions: Length: 19.47m (63ft 10in), Wingspan: 31.70m (104ft), Height: 6.15m (20ft 2in)
Powerplant: Two 890kW (1200hp) R-1830-S1C3-G radial piston engines
Maximum Speed: 315km/h (196mph)
Range: 4060km (2520 miles)
Ceiling: 4800m (15,800ft)
Crew: 9
Armament: Six 7.7mm (0.303in) guns (one in bow, four in waist blisters and one aft of the hull step); 1814kg (4,000lb) of bombs or depth charges; torpedo racks were also available

PBY Catalina Mk.IIA
This Royal Air Force Catalina Mk.IIA, number WQ-M (VA703) served with 209 Squadron on patrol duties in the Atlantic. It was part of a batch produced by Canadian Vickers.

Vought OS2U Kingfisher

The catapult-launched Kingfisher was the first production aircraft to use spot-welding. Its floats could be replaced by wheels for use from a land station.

The Kingfisher was the first catapult-launched seaplane used by the US Navy, providing vessels with a long-range reconnaissance and gunnery spotting platform and offering the possibility of rescue for downed airmen. It first flew in March 1938 and entered service in August 1940, equipping anti-submarine squadrons operating from land bases as well as major warships.

In the search-and-rescue role, the Kingfisher saved many lives. Among them was World War I ace Eddie Rickenbacker. After 24 days at sea in a dinghy, Rickenbacker and three other survivors of a B-17 crash were spotted by a Kingfisher, which picked them up but could not take off with such a heavy load. Rather than risk leaving some of the men and hoping to find them again, the Kingfisher taxied on the surface for some 64km (40 miles)

to a PT boat. Rickenbacker and his comrades rode on the wings.

Overseas service

In total, 1519 Kingfishers were built, of which 100 went to the Royal Navy. Others went to the USSR, Uruguay, Mexico, Chile and Australia. The US Navy retained some examples in service until the end of the war, though most had been phased out by then in favour of the Curtiss Seahawk. The last operator was Fidel Castro's Cuban revolutionary forces, using an example as a makeshift ground-attack platform in 1959.

Kingfisher Mk I

Australia received several Kingfishers originally intended for use by the Netherlands East Indies, putting them into RAAF service during late 1942.

Vought OS2U-3 Kingfisher

Weight: (Maximum take-off) 2722kg (6000lb)
Dimensions: Length: 10.24m (33ft 7in), Wingspan: 10.94m (35ft 11in), Height: 4.47m (14ft 8in)
Powerplant: One 340kW (450hp) Pratt & Whitney R-985-AN2 Wasp Junior 9-cylinder, air-cooled radial piston engine
Speed: 275km/h (171mph)
Range: 1461km (908 miles)
Ceiling: 5500m (18,200ft)
Crew: 2
Armament: One 7.62mm (0.3in) Browning M1919 machine gun fixed forward-firing in forward fuselage, one 7.62mm (0.3in) Browning M1919 machine gun flexibly mounted in rear cockpit; up to 295kg (650lb) bomb load

---

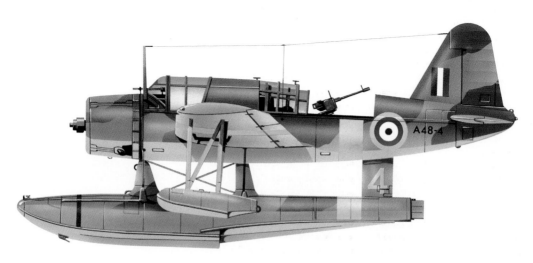

Curtiss SO3C-1 Seamew

The Seamew was developed as a replacement for the SOC Seagull and as a reconnaissance and spotting aircraft operating from the US Navy's cruisers. It was not a success.

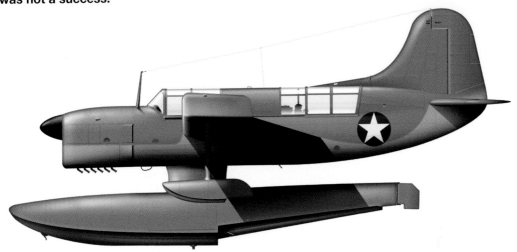

Curtiss SO3C-1 Seamew

This SO3C-1 (bureau number 4861), was assigned to the light cruiser USS *Denver* but capsized during recovery and was lost on 24 January 1941.

The initial requirement was for a folding-wing seaplane with improved range and speed compared to the preceding Seagull, to be powered by a Ranger V-770 engine. Built to this specification, the prototype XSO3C first flew in October 1939. Its competitor, the Vought XO2U-1, was superior and should have been adopted for service, but since Vought had no space manufacturing capability, the Seamew was ordered instead.

New nickname

Initially named Seagull – the same as the aircraft it was to replace – the SO3C-1 eventually came to be known by its British nickname of Seamew. It proved a troublesome aircraft, prone to instability only partially corrected by altering the tail and wingtip design, as

well as maintenance and overheating problems with the Ranger V770 engine. The first Seamew in US Navy service was taken aboard USS *Cleveland* in July 1942. A total of 300 SO3C-1s were constructed before the SO3C-2 was adopted. This variant featured catapult-launch equipment and an arrestor hook, with a wheeled undercarriage for carrier operations, and could deliver a 227kg (500lb) bomb. 452 SO3C-2s were built, of which 150 were provided to the Royal Navy. Forty-four of the SO3C-3 version, with a more powerful V-770-8 engine and no catapult equipment, were delivered. However, the overall design was over all so poor that it was replaced for catapult launch by the reinstated SOC Seagull.

Curtiss SO3C-1

Weight: (Maximum take-off) 2599kg (5729lb)

Dimensions: Length: 11.23m (36ft 10in) on floats, 10.41m (34ft 2in) on wheels, Wingspan: 11.58m (38ft), Height: 4.57m (15ft)

Powerplant: One 450kW (600hp) Ranger V-770-6 inverted V12 air-cooled piston engine

Speed: 277km/h (172mph)

Range: 1850km (1150 miles)

Ceiling: 4800m (15,800ft)

Crew: 2

Armament: One 7.62mm (0.3in) M1919 Browning machine gun fixed forward-firing; one 12.7mm (0.5in) M2 Browning machine gun flexibly mounted in rear cockpit; two 45kg (100lb) bombs or 147kg (325lb) depth charges under wings

Index

Picture Credits

Photos

AirSeaLandPhotos: 7
Amber Books: 6, 8, 18, 23, 40, 57, 62, 71, 75
Getty: 101 (Corbis), 104 (Photo12/Universal Images Group), 111 (Keystone)
Naval History & Heritage Command: 46, 80, 83, 92, 95, 98, 107, 115, 117, 118
Public Domain: 48, 102
U.S. National Museum of Naval Aviation: 84

Artworks

Amber Books: 10, 15, 19–21 all, 26 both, 28/29, 31, 35–39 all, 41–45 all, 50–56 all, 59, 61, 63 all, 68–70 all, 73, 75, 77, 82, 83, 87–91 all, 93–94 all, 96–97 all, 99, 106, 112–116 all, 119–122 all
David Bocquelet: 85, 100, 103
Ed Jackson (www.artbyedo.com): 11–13 all, 16–17 all, 74, 76, 78, 79, 108–109 all
Rolando Ugolini: 5, 24–25, 27 both, 30, 32, 33, 49, 64–67 all, 71
Teasel Studios: 123